This book is dedicated
to all the dogs that
make our lives richer
every day.

1,001 Reasons to Love™

Dogs

Christine Miele & Mary Tiegreen

Stewart, Tabori & Chang
New York

Published in 2006 by Stewart, Tabori & Chang
An imprint of Harry N. Abrams, Inc.

Library of Congress Cataloging-in-Publication Data

Miele, Christine.
  1,001 reasons to love dogs / Christine Miele & Mary Tiegreen.
    p. cm.
  ISBN-13: 978-1-58479-526-1
  ISBN-10: 1-58479-526-3
  1. Dogs—Miscellanea. 2. Dogs—Pictorial works. I. Tiegreen, Mary.
II. Title. III. Title: One thousand one reasons to love dogs.

SF426.2M53 2006
636.7—dc22

2006010314

Editor: Jennifer Levesque
Designer: Mary Tiegreen
Production Manager: Kim Tyner

1,001 Reasons to Love Dogs is a book in the
1,001 REASONS TO LOVE™ Series.

1,001 REASONS TO LOVE™ is a trademark of
Mary Tiegreen and Hubert Pedroli.

The text of this book was composed in ITC Cheltenham Condensed, Adriatic, Goudy, and Powhatten.

Printed and bound in China
10 9 8 7 6 5 4 3 2

HNA ▮▮▮▮▮
harry n. abrams, inc.
a subsidiary of La Martinière Groupe

115 West 18th Street
New York, NY 10011
www.hnabooks.com

CONTENTS

Dusty

Introduction

One of the happiest days in my childhood was going to visit the breeder with my father to pick out a Wire Fox Terrier puppy. I sat on the floor in the breeder's living room surrounded by all these squiggly puppies licking my face. A few weeks later we brought home Chips, who would become the terror of the neighborhood. In those pre-leash-law times, his favorite pastimes were digging up the neighbor's flower garden and following my grandmother to the butcher shop. In spite of his indomitable spirit, Chips was a therapy dog par excellence, making hospital rounds and house calls with my father. They were inseparable.

Even at that young age, I always considered it a badge of honor if the dog chose to sleep in my bed rather than my sister's. I kept asking for more dogs, but while my father was in favor of it, we always were vetoed, so I had to wait until I grew up.

After college I was always the first to volunteer when a friend needed a dogsitter and so became acquainted with Labs, Bijons, Lhasas, and a very special Golden Retriever. My canine education began in earnest with our Golden, Dusty. He started me on a road to being a trainer and truly understanding life from a dog's point of view.

I met Mary Tiegreen many years ago when she was looking for a puppy. Someone told her that I had a litter of puppies out of two of my Champion Goldens. She adopted her beloved Daisy from me, and we became friends.

This book has been a wonderful adventure. Each day has been filled with friendships, fun, and amazement at the generosity of my longtime dog friends and the new ones I have just met.

When I reflect on the most important reason for me, I can honestly say that my life would not be complete without my beloved dogs. The most important reason is that they have taught me to recognize love.

—*Christine Miele*

The Perfect Dog

"The eyes of a dog, the expression of a dog, the warmly wagging tail of a dog and the gloriously cold damp nose of a dog were in my opinion all God-given for one purpose only—to make complete fools of human beings."

—*Barbara Woodhouse*

1
Love, loyalty, devotion,
friendship, and a single
trusting heart

Dogs Are More Than the Sum of Their Parts

From head to tail, dogs are love bundled in fur.

2 The range of expression in a dog's eyes

3 An old dog's white eyelashes

4 The full, round eyes of the Chihuahua

5 The haw eyes of the Bloodhound

6 The intent gaze of a dog on alert

7 Looking away when confronted

8 Being submissive when accused of wrongdoing

9 The China blue eyes of the Siberian Husky

10 The ghostly gray eyes of the Weimaraner

11 The expressiveness of one raised eyebrow

12 A dog's eyes are a window to the soul

13 The intense connection when a dog peers into your soul

14
The dark-rimmed eyes
of the Pembroke
Welsh Corgi

"The spaniel heart is warm. The soft spaniel eye brims with love. If ever the world's diplomats and arms negotiators learn the spaniel gaze, there will be peace on earth."

—*Larry Shook*

15
The soft look of friendship and welcome

The amazing sensitivity of a dog's nose

29
The functional
design and
incredible variety
of dogs' ears

30
The marvelous, multifunctional dog's tongue, used for tasting, lapping, cooling the body, cleaning one's fur, and kissing

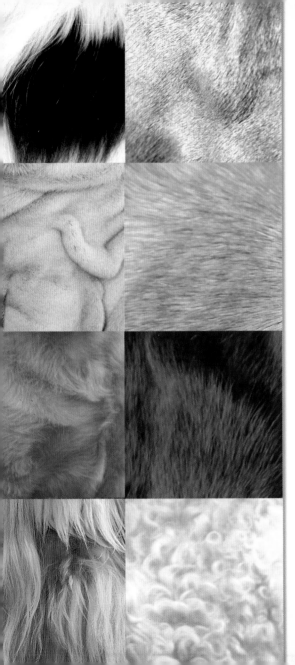

23

53
The thick coat of the Malamute, as warm as down on a winter's day

54
Dogs with hair instead of fur: Poodles, Portuguese Water Dogs, and Bichon Frises

55 The art of removing chewing gum from dog fur

If you catch it right away, gum not yet entwined in the coat can be frozen with an ice cube and broken apart. If the gum is matted into the coat, rub the area with peanut butter and it will be easy to remove.

56 A tried-and-true de-skunking method

Do not wet the dog. Prepare a paste of one bottle of hydrogen peroxide, ⅔ cup of baking soda, and 1 tablespoon of liquid dishwashing soap. Add 1 cup of white vinegar for more serious cases. Sponge it on the spot and let it sit for about 10 minutes, refresh it, and rub it in some more. Rinse and dry.

57
A feathered
tail

58
A curly little tail

60
Swashbuckling
whip tails

59
A question mark
spiral tail

61
Tails with attitude

62
The beautiful plumed tail
of the Japanese Chin

70 Paw prints in mud, snow, wet sand—and across the kitchen floor

71 The compact "cat feet" of the Doberman Pinscher

Some dogs have "cat feet," rounded compact ones with toes all about the same length. This type of foot, which requires less energy to lift, is seen on the Doberman Pinscher and Giant Schnauzer.

72 Hare feet

Some dogs have "hare feet," which resemble the rabbit's foot: the two middle toes are longer than the outside two. This can be found on many of the toy breeds and coursing breeds, such as Greyhounds and Salukis.

73 The webbed feet of the water dogs

Dogs bred for water activities, such as the Chesapeake Bay Retriever, Portuguese Water Dog, and Golden Retriever, have webbed feet to help them swim.

74 The biomechanics of digging

A dog is specially equipped for digging, with sturdy pads and strong claws.

75
A dog's paws smell like fresh popcorn

Dogs perspire through their feet and have scent
glands on the bottom of their paws that
resemble the aroma of popcorn.

A Breed Apart

Dogs come in so many varieties, each having its own
unique characteristics to love.

85
The unique gaze of the Australian Shepherd, with
one blue eye and
one brown eye

GRAND MASTER
CHAMPION
SAN BERNARD

94
The kind temperament of
the Labrador Retriever

95
The wrinkles of the Chinese Shar-Pei

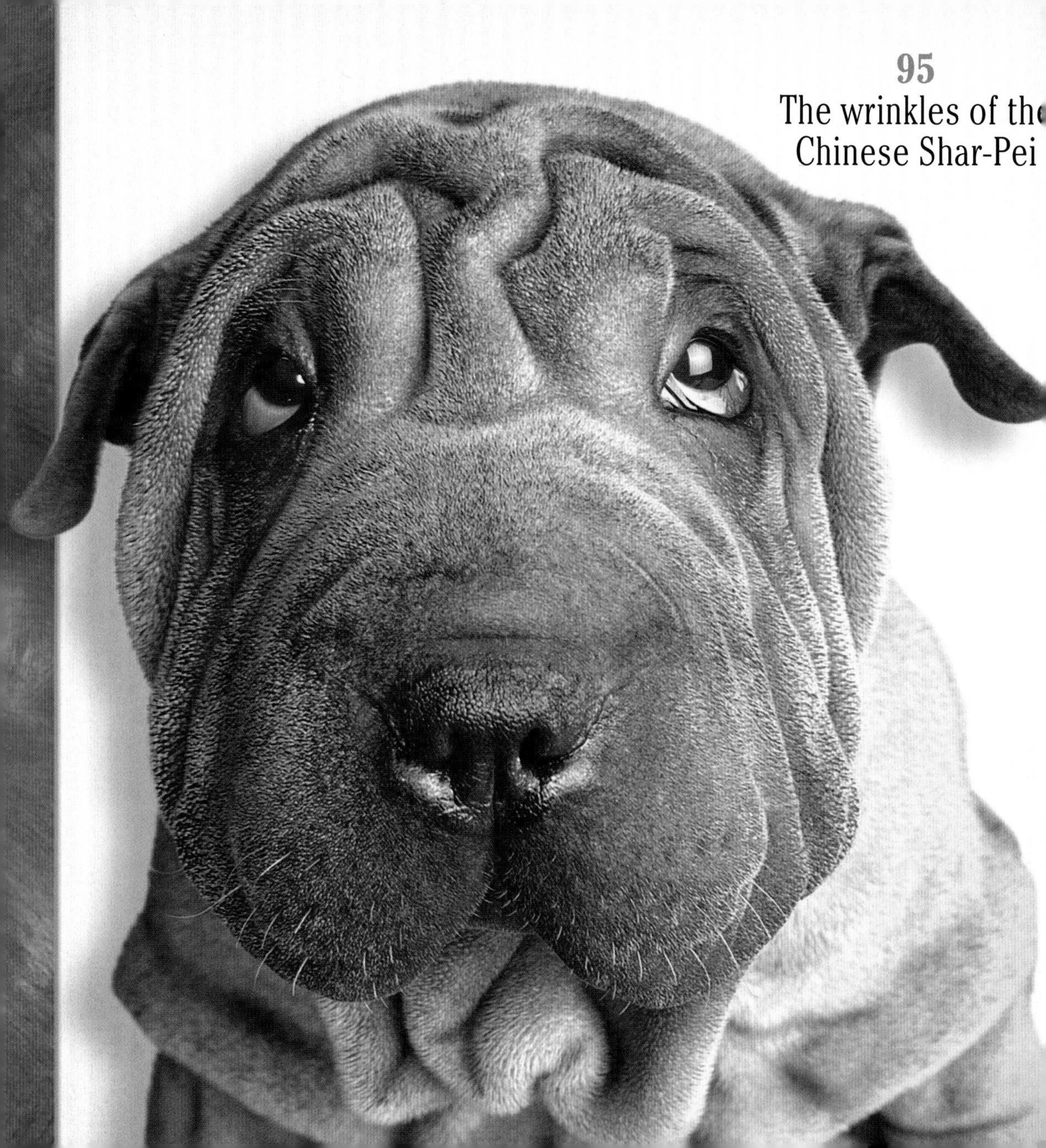

136
The exuberance of the
Shetland Sheepdog

137
The butterfly ears of
the Papillon

145
The total
happiness of the
Golden Retriever

161
The Winston Churchill look of the Bulldog

"An Airedale can do anything any other dog can do and then whip the other dog if he has to."
—*Theodore Roosevelt*

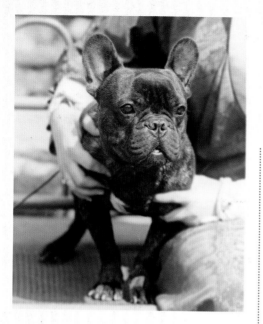

181
Having the ears of the French Bulldog

"Things that upset a terrier may pass virtually unnoticed by a Great Dane."

—Anonymous

201 The bold independence of the Parson Russell Terrier

202 The reliability of the Staffordshire Bull Terrier

203 Thinking you can fly like the Pemboke Welsh Corgi

204 The utilitarian good looks of the Welsh Terrier

205 Being bold enough to tree a bear: the Plott Hound

206 The "chrysanthemum-faced" Shih Tzu

207 The grace, power, and speed of the Pharaoh Hound

208 The Polish Lowland Sheepdog, sometimes nicknamed PON after his Polish name, "Polski Owczarek Nizinny"

209 The fisherman's robust dog: the Portuguese Water Dog

210 The pleading eyes of the Redbone Coonhound

211 The ridge of the Rhodesian Ridgeback

212 The grace of the Saluki

213 The hazel eyes of the Sussex Spaniel

214 Herding reindeer: the Samoyed

215 Being an alert guardian like the Schipperke

216 The ground-covering stride of the Scottish Deerhound

217 Being able to swim like a Newfoundland

218 The spirit of the Sealyham Terrier

219 Being trusted by Sergeant Preston of the Yukon: the Siberian Husky

220 The endurance of the Wirehaired Pointing Griffon

221
The confidence of
the West Highland
White Terrier

222
The charm of
the Pug

> "The Pug is living proof
> that God has a
> sense of humor."
> —*Margot Kaufman*

Dogs in Art

From ancient cave drawings to Wegman's Weimaraners, artists have shared with us their insights into the world of dogs.

234 The dogs of ancient artists
Images of dogs can be found in cave paintings thousands of years old. In the tombs of Egypt, specific breeds of dogs such as the Pharaoh Hound and Saluki are depicted.

A 4,000-year-old painting from the Valley of the Kings, Egypt

235 A glimpse of royalty with their dogs
George Stubbs (1724-1806) earned his reputation as a painter of horses, along with his illustrations for *The Anatomy of the Horse*. He painted for the landed gentry and royalty, specializing in portraits, as well as images of dogs in the field.

236 The softness the dog gives to the monarch
Sir Edwin Landseer(1802-1873), Queen Victoria's favorite artist, had his first exhibition at the Royal Academy in London at the age of 13. His father and his brother Thomas were engravers, so many of his works were sold as prints, to a broad audience. By the age of 15, he was a regular exhibitor at the Royal Academy.

237 A life-size painting of the Saint Bernard
Maud Earl (1864–1943) started in the world of dog shows and purebred dogs in England. In the late 19th century, new breeds were being established among dog devotees. She enjoyed the patronage of Queen Victoria and of the Prince and Princess of Wales, Albert and Alexandra. Her famous painting *I Hear a Voice*, depicting the magnificent Saint Bernard English Champion Frandley Stephanie, hangs in the lobby of the American Kennel Club's New York City offices.

A Dog Looking
Out of a Kennel,
by Edwin Landseer.
Oil on canvas.
Courtesy of William
Secord Gallery, Inc.,
New York

238
The perfect representation of the Terrier in oil

Arthur Wardle (1864–1949) had a unique combination of being an accomplished artist while having a great sensitivity and understanding of purebred dogs. His famous paintings of the Totteridge Kennels Smooth Fox Terriers were reproduced as fine-art prints.

In addition, 250 of his paintings were reproduced on cigarette cards, 80 of his watercolors and paintings were reproduced on postcards, and Spratt's reproduced 36 of his images on cards.

The Intruder, by Arthur Wardle. Oil on canvas. From the collection of the American Kennel Club Museum of the Dog

55

239
Denis Springer's sculpture

Springer was a professional dog handler and recognized authority on terriers. In 1990, he began sculpting dogs. Today, his bronze and pewter works are highly collectible. Denis is the artist who created the Golden Retriever Club of America Excellence in Agility Trophy, modeled after Champion Cross Creek Tippicanoe, OA.

Susan Bahary's sculpture
Always Faithful

Susan Bahary, a former breeder, is renowned for her bronze and acrylic equine and canine sculptures. One of her most famous works is the Doberman Pinscher sculpture *Always Faithful*, the official national monument for the World War II U.S. Marine Corps service dogs. A replica of this statue is at the University of Tennessee's College of Veterinary Medicine in Knoxville. In October 2002, Ms. Bahary completed a tribute to the California law-enforcement dog, a German Shepherd statue titled *Faithful Partner*, which stands in front of the University of California at Davis School of Veterinary Medicine.

*Always Faithful, by Susan Bahary.
Bronze. From the collection of the
American Kennel Club Museum of the*

241
Morgan Dennis

One of the most prolific illustrators in modern times, Dennis is best known for his drawings of Scottish Terriers for the Black and White Scotch Whiskey ads and the ads for Pard Dog Food. He is considered an expert at representing the inquisitive and mischievous nature of his subjects.

BASEBALL
TODAY

Hearth's Delight

242
The illustrations of Lucy Dawson

Lucy Dawson, whose pseudonym was "Mac," worked in pen and ink, oils, and pastels, creating charming illustrations that captured the spirit and character of dogs. With simple backgrounds and limited color palette, the focus of each drawing is the expression of the dog. Dawson's work appeared on Wills Cigarette Cards, in books, and on postcards from Valentine's and Sons during the 1930s. Her book *Dogs as I See Them* was published in 1937.

243
Bonzo

JUST MANAGING TO KEEP THINGS GOING !

Artist George Studdy started drawing the dog that would become Bonzo in 1912, and Bonzo became a regular in *The Sketch* magazine starting in 1921. The adorable dog with one black ear and one white ear was an instant hit and went on to become a worldwide success in books, cards, games, toys, automobile hood ornaments, and all forms of advertising and promotional items. Bonzo appeared in a total of 26 animated films, the first of which, *A Sausage Sensation*, premiered in London in October 1924. The premiere was attended by King George V and Queen Mary, the first time a reigning sovereign had gone to the movies in a public cinema.

A Leg Pull.

244 The endearing illustrations of Marguerite Kirmse

Kirmse (1885–1954) was born in England, graduated from the Royal Academy of Music as a harpist, and then migrated to America. An artist of many talents, she is best known for her pastels and etchings. In addition, she illustrated several of Albert Payson Terhune's books and created a series of bronzes that are highly prized collectibles today. Kirmse bred Scottish Terriers in Connecticut under the kennel name of Tobermory.

happy New Year

1937 · JANUARY · 1937

SUNDAY	MONDAY	TUESDAY	WEDNESDAY	THURSDAY	FRIDAY	SATURDAY
We Resolve to: • SAVE YOU MONEY • SELL YOU THE BEST PRODUCTS …and give you the BEST SERVICE				Last Quar. 4th New Moon 12th First Quar. 19th Full Moon 26th	1	2
3	4	5	6	7	8	9
10	11	12	13	14	15	16
17	18	19	20	21	22	23
24 31	25	26	27	28	29	30

1936 DECEMBER 1936

SUN	MON	TUE	WED	THU	FRI	SAT
L.Q.5	N.M.13	1	2	3	4	5
6	7	8	9	10	11	12
13	14	15	16	17	18	19
20	21	22	23	24	25	26
27	28	29	30	31	F.Q.21	F.M.27

1937 FEBRUARY 1937

SUN	MON	TUE	WED	THU	FRI	SAT
	1	2	3	4	5	6
7	8	9	10	11	12	13
14	15	16	17	18	19	20
21	22	23	24	25	26	27
28	L.Q.3	N.M.11	F.Q.17	F.M.25		

245 William Wegman

Photographer Wegman began an inventive partnership with his famous Weimaraner, Man Ray, using a 20-by-24-inch Polaroid camera. Man Ray enjoyed celebrity status for his gray presence and Weimaraner antics, coupled with the imagination of the artist. In 1986, Fay Ray was born, and Wegman continues his exploration of the dog with her offspring. He is considered the master of many media, including photography, film, video, and television.

246 Blue Dog

In 1984, Louisiana artist George Rodrigue created Blue Dog for a book of Cajun ghost stories. Inspired by photos of his dog Tiffany, who had died some years before, he placed the dog in an eerie graveyard setting and titled the painting *Loup Garou*. He would go on to paint Blue Dog for years to come.

247

The art of Stephen Huneck

Vermont artist Stephen Huneck had the inspiration
to do a series of woodcuts based on his black Lab,
Sally. Then tragedy struck. In 1994, Huneck went
into a two-month coma after falling down a flight of
stairs. Upon his recovery he began the series with the
first woodcut, titled *Life Is a Ball,* a celebration of his
newfound life. He works with a collection of over
150 chisels, 30 planes, and axes. His woodcuts are
whimsical and full of heart and humor, yet there is
a much deeper emotional response in those who
view them. Huneck has done several books, and his
main gallery is located in Woodstock, Vermont.
Not far from his home are Dog Mountain and
his wonderful Dog Chapel.

IS A BALL

Ultramarine

Patience

Tillamook Cheddar

Tillamook Cheddar

Afterbirth
Nov. 2 – 15

Black & White
new works on suede and paper
opening October 18, 2001

Geronimo

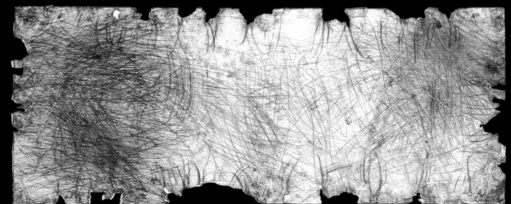

248
The artist Tillamook Cheddar

This talented Jack Russell Terrier from Brooklyn, New York, is widely regarded as the world's preeminent canine artist. Her medium is a dynamic color transfer technique using pigment-coated vellum and lithograph paper. Working with claws and teeth, she creates works of drama and raw emotion that most human abstract painters can only dream of. Her work has been displayed in museums and galleries in New York, Belgium, and Amsterdam.

"SHE WORKS WITH HOCKING INTENSITY, SOMETIMES TO THE OINT OF DESTROYING HER CREATIONS."

—tillamookcheddar.com

Remember My Name

Dogs have been with us throughout history, and several have achieved mythic status through heroism, companionship, loyalty, or just plain good looks.

249 Black Shuck

Black Shuck, whose name comes from *soucca*, Anglo-Saxon for "Satan," was a phantom dog that roamed the countryside in England, terrifying the population for hundreds of years. No one actually dared to look at the dog, since the belief was that this would result in death, but people would become aware of his presence through a feeling. It was said that he was as big as a calf, with a shaggy black coat and large eyes that burned like hot coals. In East Anglia, when a person is bad-tempered it is said that "the black dog's walked over him," and of one who is dying, "The black dog is at his heels." Black Shuck is said to have been the inspiration for Sir Arthur Conan Doyle's *The Hound of the Baskervilles*.

250 Argos

Odysseus's faithful dog, Argos, waited for twenty years for his master's return, while most people presumed that he had died in the Trojan War. Upon his return, Odysseus was disguised as a beggar and only Argos recognized his master.

251 Cavall (aka Cafall, Cabal)

King Arthur's favorite hunting dog was a symbol of loyalty, skill, and self-sacrifice and was treated with the respect given to a warrior. Legend has it that during a famous hunt for a large boar, Cavall left a paw print on a stone and Arthur placed a pile of stones below it, creating a cairn, or a mound of stones placed as a memorial. Today,

on a mountain known as Carn Cavall in Wales, is a stone with an oval indentation rounded at the bottom that resembles a dog's footprint.

252 Sirius, the Dog Star
(Alpha Canis Majoris)
Residing in the constellation Canis Major, or the Big Dog, representing Orion's larger hunting dog, Sirius is the brightest star in the sky. Only 8.5 light-years away, this bright star is 25 times more luminous than our sun. In ancient times, the rising of Sirius, whose name derived from the Greek word *Seirius*, meaning "searing" or "scorching," heralded the rising of the Nile and the beginning of "the dog days of summer."

Napoleon's companion in exile is preserved, along with his horse, at the Musée de l'Armée in Paris.

253 The Dog of the Seven Sleepers

This faithful dog accompanied his masters to the cave near Ephesus where they were confined, and stood by them without food, water, or sleep for nearly 300 years. The story was immortalized in a poem by Goethe.

254 Cerberus

The three-headed dog who guarded the underworld, he was subdued by Heracles.

255 Saur, Dog King of Norway

During the 11th century, a dog named Saur was proclaimed king of Norway by his master, the previously deposed and reinstated king. Saur "ruled" for three years and was treated in royal fashion.

256 Fortune, the fortunate Pug of Empress Josephine

Napoleon Bonaparte was never fond of dogs, and on his wedding night he was forced to share the bed with his new wife's Pug, Fortune. Perhaps in defense of his mistress, during lovemaking Fortune went into attack mode and sank his teeth into Napoleon's naked calf, with the resulting scar being one he carried for the remainder of his life. Not all of Fortune's actions were destructive, however. Before her marriage to Napoleon, Josephine was imprisoned during the French Revolution. She was able to pass messages to those who could help save her by tucking notes under Fortune's wide velvet collar.

257 Napoleon's dog on Elba

This long-legged white dog was Napoleon's companion during his first exile, on Elba.

258 Rigel, hero of the *Titanic* disaster

Rigel, the Newfoundland owned by Lieutenant William Murdock, first officer of the *Titanic*, was said to have saved many lives after the sinking of the ship. He was in the water for hours, looking for his master who had gone down with the ship. In the darkness, the rescue ship, *Carpathia*, almost ran into one of the lifeboats, but crewmen heard Rigel barking, alerting them to the position of the lifeboat below their starboard bow, and the passengers were saved.

259 Seaman, Lewis and Clark's Newfoundland

Captain Meriwether Lewis led the explorers from the beginning of the expedition, in 1803. Lewis was offered three beaver skins for his beloved dog. He refused, writing in his journal that "I prised much for his docility and qualifications generally for my journey and of course there was no bargain."

260 Greyfriars Bobby

In 1858, a man named John Gray died in Edinburgh, Scotland, and was buried in the old Greyfriars Churchyard. For the next fourteen years, Bobby, this man's faithful Skye Terrier, kept watch over the grave, leaving only for his midday meal at one o'clock each day. The dog remained faithful until his own death in 1872. A statue was erected outside the churchyard to commemorate this extraordinary act of devotion.

261 Hachiko

This Japanese Akita, owned by a professor in Tokyo, would meet his master at the train station each evening when he returned from work, to escort him home. The professor died in 1925, but Hachiko continued to return to the station each evening and wait for his missing master for the next nine years. Upon Hachiko's death, a bronze statue was erected at the west exit of the Shibuya station to honor and commemorate his faithfulness.

262 Patsy Ann, "the Official Greeter of Juneau, Alaska"

Patsy Ann, a Bull Terrier born in 1929, was always found at wharfside to welcome visitors as the ships arrived in port. Although she was deaf from birth, she sensed the approaching ships before they appeared on the horizon and would trot off to the dock. During her life she was quite well known and well loved. Fifty years after her death in 1942, a statue was commissioned by the "Friends of Patsy Ann." Artist Anna Burke Harris included clippings of dog hair from all over the world in the bronze statue, which was unveiled on July 3, 1992. Legend has it that if you greet Patsy Ann and gently give her a touch, you will "carry with you the blessings of friendship through your life's journey."

"Love is patient, love is kind, ❧ Love does not insist on its own way. ❧ Love bears all things, believes all things, hopes all things, endures all things. ❧ Love never fails."
—I Corinthians 13:4–8

Greyfriars Bobby

"SHEP, FORT BENTON'S FAMOUS DOG"

263 Old Shep

In the summer of 1936, a sheepherder, accompanied by his dog, Shep, arrived in Fort Benton, Montana, seeking treatment for an illness. The poor man died several days later, and his body was loaded on a train to be sent back to his family in the East. The dog followed the casket to the train but wasn't allowed to board.

For the next five years, Shep arrived at the station each day to greet four trains in hopes that his master would be on board. He became known across America, thanks to being featured in "Ripley's Believe It or Not," and began receiving gifts and fan mail. On January 12, 1942, Shep was struck by a train and died. His obituary was carried on the AP and UPI wire services, and hundreds attended his funeral. In 1994, Fort Benton dedicated a bronze statue by famous sculptor Bob Scriver of Shep, depicted with his two front paws on a train rail, waiting.

"A dog is the only thing on earth that loves you more than he loves himself."

—Josh Billings

264 Owney, the postal service mascot

Owney, a mixed breed, was found in Albany in 1888 outside the post office. The postal workers brought him inside, where he fell asleep on a pile of empty mailbags. Apparently he was comforted by the scent of mail, since he followed the bags onto mail trains and traveled across the state—and eventually across the country. Wherever he stopped, Owney was given a new tag. Eventually Postmaster General John Wanamaker gave Owney a special jacket on which to display his tags.

In 1895, Owney made a trip around the world, traveling with mailbags bound for Asia and Europe. Upon his death in 1897, mail clerks raised the money to have him preserved, and today he resides at the Smithsonian Institution, in the National Postal Museum's atrium, proudly wearing his jacket full of tags.

265
Balto

In January 1925, a deadly diphtheria epidemic was threatening to reach Nome, Alaska. The only available serum for prevention of the disease was 1,000 miles away in Anchorage. The vaccine could not be shipped by air because of the onset of the difficult Alaskan winter, so it was decided to use dog sleds to transport the medicine. The sled teams had to endure blizzards with temperatures below −50 degrees Fahrenheit and extremely high winds.

Balto, a Siberian Husky, was the lead sled dog on Gunnar Kaasen's team. His was the final team transporting the diphtheria antitoxin. Just six days after the serum left Anchorage, the team rode down the streets of Nome with Balto in the lead. His face soon became known around the world; the following year, a statue of Balto was installed in New York's Central Park.

After his lifesaving event, Balto was sold and went to Hollywood, where he made a movie but eventually wound up, undernourished and abused, at a "dime-a-look" sideshow in Los Angeles. Then a Cleveland businessman, after having seen the sickening display of the entire dog-sled team, launched a campaign in his home city to raise money to purchase the dogs. The "Balto fund" raised $2,000 in less than ten days, and the entire team of dogs—Balto, Tillie, Fox, Sye, Billy, Old Moctoc, and Alaska Slim—were relocated to Cleveland's zoo, where they lived out their days.

Balto died in 1933 at the age of 11. His body was preserved and is now on display at Cleveland's Natural History Museum as a reminder of his heroic race to save the children of Nome.

"There's more
to life than
being really,
really good
looking."
—Derek Zoolander

Handsome Dan XVI

266 Handsome Dan, the Yale Bulldog

The popular Yale mascot got his start in 1889, when undergraduate Andrew B. Graves purchased a bulldog from a New

Haven blacksmith for $5. Before each game, he was led across the field, and he became the first mascot of any university in the United States. The *Hartford Courant* wrote that "he seemed like a cross between an alligator and a horned frog" and that "he was always taken to games on a leash, and the Harvard football team for years owed its continued existence to the fact that the rope held." Upon his death in 1898, his body was preserved and today resides in Yale's Payne Whitney Gymnasium. Nearly 35 years would pass before Handsome Dan II came on the scene. In April 2005, Mugsy, a 69-pound Bulldog from Hamden, Connecticut, was chosen to be Handsome Dan XVI.

267 Laika *(Barker)*, Bars *(Panther or Lynx)*, Lisichka *(Little Fox)*, Belka *(Squirrel)*, Strelka *(Little Arrow)*, Pchelka *(Little Bee)*, Mushka *(Little Fly)*, Damka *(Little Lady)*, Krasavka *(Beauty)*, Chernushka *(Blackie)*, Zvezdochka *(Little Star)*, Verterok *(Little Wind)*, and Ugolyok *(Little Piece of Coal)*

These are the dogs of the early Russian space program. Laika, the first dog to orbit the Earth, is remembered with a monument in Star City, near Moscow. Belka and Strelka were the first animals to survive orbital flight. (Strelka went on to have a litter of six puppies, one of whom was given to Caroline Kennedy as a gift from Nikita

Belka and Strelka

Khrushchev.) Verterok and Ugolyok set a record by staying in orbit for 22 days. The total time in space was not exceeded until Skylab 2 in June 1974.

268 Toby

This Standard Poodle was said to be the richest dog in the world after he was left $75 million by his wealthy owner, Ella Wendel, in 1931.

Rusty, the Comfort Dog

Rusty is a certified comfort dog who visits schools, hospitals, and nursing homes bringing companionship and joy to those in need. With his owner, Carl Maier, Rusty was there during the tragic days after September 11, offering comfort to those who had lost children, parents, and friends. His quiet presence and giving heart encouraged them to hug him and cry into his ruff.

Not only is Rusty is a direct descendant of Lassie, and the son of the eighth Weatherwax "Lassie," he is the official American Red Cross mascot. Rusty helped to raise money for the Hurrican Relief Fund and is a true lifesaver with his dedicated owner.

Carl Maier's original Collie, Lucky, was one of Albert Payson Terhune's Sunnybank Collies and the subject of a beautiful children's book *The Collie of Castle Hill*. Ever since the day Lucky saved him from drowning in the river, Carl has always understood the depth of love we share with dogs and, through his work with Rusty, has been generous in sharing this with others.

Rusty, photographed
Sue Akin and Donald
Fowler, akin-fowler.c

Арап.

Арлекин.

Август.

Байкал

Карб...

Бек.

Икар.

Чингис Хан.

Дружо...

Леди

Журка.

Джек.

Бокс.

Икс.

ызун,

Джой.

Черный.

Диана.

270
Pavlov's dogs

Although Russian scientist Ivan Pavlov was the first to describe the psychological situation known as classical conditioning, his experiment had actually begun as a study of digestion. During his work with dogs, he noticed that they began to salivate even before food was presented to them. In order to stimulate salivation in his dogs, Pavlov used not only bells but also whistles, tuning forks, metronomes, and visual cues. The experiments, done in the late 1800s and early 1900s, were first published in English in 1927. However, very little was known about the individual dogs until nearly 70 years later. In 1992, Professor Tim Tully of the Cold Spring Harbor Laboratory was invited to lecture at the Pavlov Institute in Koltushi. Tully was interested in finding out the identities of the dogs in order to name the subjects in his own experiments on fruit flies. On the last day of his extended visit, he was invited to tour Pavlov's home. It was there that Dr. Nonna Volkova, the curator, brought out a photo album that had been presented to Pavlov by his students for his 83rd birthday. In it were 40 of the dogs, with their Russian names inscribed below.

Красавец.

Мартик.

Милорд.

Новичек.

Милка.

Умница.

Норд.

Молодец.

Пингель.

Злодей.

Рыжий.

Валет.

Рыжий.

Пострел.

Мурашка.

Ласка.

PAVLOV'S DOGS

Valiet-1	Ruslan	Molodietz
Tungus	Milkah-2	Milord-2
Iks	Murashka-1	Barbos-2
Umnitza	Bely-1	Dikar
Valiet-2	Rex	Nord
Barbos-1	Mampus	Drujok
Laska	Novichok	Trezor
Valiet-3	Mirta	Jurka
Ikar	Pingiel	Jack
Rogdai	Bely-2	Murashka-2
Arleekin	Rijiy I	Martik
Krasavietz	Diana	Premjera
Postrel	Milord-1	Joy
Norka	Zolotisty	Visgun
Beck-1	Rosa	Arap
Beck-2	Gryzun	Zlodey
Toi	Chingis Khan	Rijiy II
Rafael	Chyorny	Lis
Milkah-1	Baikal	Lady
Avgust	Box	John

Норка

Той

Рогдай

Рекс.

Руслан.

Тунгус.

Mr. Winkle

A tiny dog resembling a teddy bear, with a prominent pink tongue and enormous dark, expressive eyes, Mr. Winkle is truly one of a kind. Rescued from an industrial area by award-winning photographer Lara Jo Regan, Mr. Winkle rose to stardom in 2001 with Regan's calendar titled "What is Mr. Winkle?" launched on mrwinkle.com. Books, cards, plush toys, media appearances, and worldwide recognition were to follow. Mr. Winkle has

become the poster boy for adopted strays, representing all their potential and all the love, happiness, and magic they can bring into our lives.

Called "The Cutest Dog in the World" by the national media, he has graced the covers of *Animal Wellness*, *Pet Life*, and *Time Magazine for Kids*, and has been written up in major newspapers from

L.A. to London. He sparked a wave of Winklemania across the globe, thanks in part to mrwinkle.com, one of the most popular websites in the history of the Internet, garnering over 65 million hits and counting. Mr. Winkle even landed a cameo on the cable TV series *Sex and the City*, playing himself at a book signing.

Moving back to her roots in documentary photography, Lara Jo Regan has made Mr. Winkle the subject of her latest gallery show, "Mr. Winkle Hotel-Motel Nudes," which opened in Los Angeles in 2006. Of her work, Regan says, "I've always been drawn to the holiness and humor of the mundane in the American landscape, and having the opportunity to evoke this with my beloved muse Mr. Winkle as tour guide was a rich thrill."

Photographs on this page are from the "What is Mr. Winkle?" series. All images © Lara Jo Regan

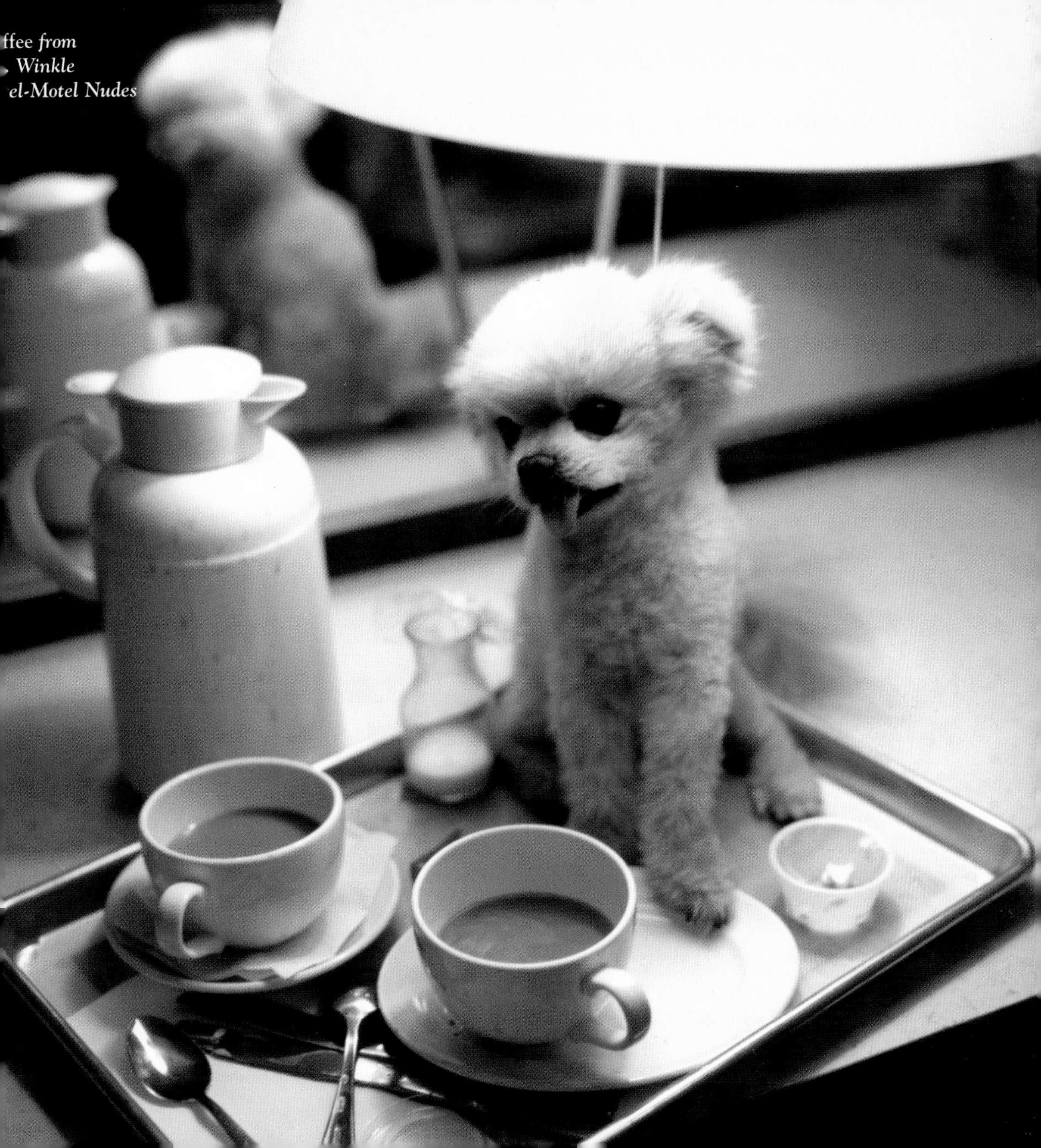

ffee from
Winkle
el-Motel Nudes

The Literary Dog

From children's books to the classics, stories with
dogs enrich our reading experience.

272 Flush

Virginia Woolf tells the story of a Spaniel
who is the companion of poet Elizabeth
Barrett while she is confined to her sick-
bed. Both their lives are transformed
when they go off to Italy and escape the
confinements of British society. Allowed
to run and explore in Florence, Flush
discovers the joy that comes with
freedom.

273 Shakespeare's dogs

In several plays, Shakespeare mentions
dogs, specifically Spaniels, Beagles,
Greyhounds, mongrels, curs, and hounds.

274 Nana

A motherly Newfoundland who takes
care of the Darling children in J. M.
Barrie's *Peter Pan*. Unable to afford a
nanny, the Darlings acquire Nana,
whom they encountered in Kensington
Gardens, where "she spent most of her
time peeping into perambulators."
The character of Nana was inspired
by Barrie's own dog, Luath.

275 *Travels with Charley*

John Steinbeck's tale of his trip around
America with Charley, his Poodle and
constant companion.

276 The Hound of the Baskervilles

The giant dog that menaced the
Baskervilles in Arthur Conan Doyle's
classic Sherlock Holmes tale. In the
1939 film version, the title role was
played by a 140-pound Great Dane
named Chief.

277 Auld Pepper, Auld Mustard, Young Pepper, Young Mustard, Little Pepper, and Little Mustard

Sir Walter Scott's 1812 novel, *Guy
Mannering*, featured a farmer named
Dandie Dinmont, who had six Terriers.
Following the popularity of the book,
the breed was forever after called
Dandie Dinmont Terriers.

278 Milou

The faithful companion of Tintin in
the series of Belgian children's books.
In English, Milou's name is Snowy.

"Outside of a dog, a book is a man's best friend. Inside of a dog, it's too dark to read."
— Groucho Marx

Buck, the courageous dog in
Jack London's *The Call of the Wild*

The Call of the Wild, written in 1903, tells the story of Buck, a large dog from a comfortable home in California who is stolen and sent to Alaska to become a sled dog during the Yukon's Gold Rush. It is an emotional tale of the struggle for survival, and the primitive instincts in us all. However, amid the drama and harsh life, London's love of animals comes through in his descriptions of the bond between Buck and his master.

E HAD A WAY OF TAKING BUCK'S HEAD ROUGHLY BETWEEN HIS HANDS, AND RESTING HIS OWN HEAD UPON BUCK'S, of shaking him back and forth, the while calling him ill names that to Buck were love names. Buck knew no greater joy than that rough embrace and the sound of murmured oaths, and at each jerk back and forth it seemed that his heart would be shaken out of his body, so great was its ecstasy. . . . ❦ For the most part, however, Buck's love was expressed in adoration. While he went wild with happiness when Thornton touched him or spoke to him, he did not seek these tokens. Unlike Skeet, who was wont to shove her nose under Thornton's hand and nudge and nudge till petted, or Nig, who would stalk up and rest his great head on Thornton's knee, Buck was content to adore at a distance. He would lie by the hour, eager, alert, at Thornton's feet, looking up into his face, dwelling upon it, studying it, following with keenest interest each fleeting expression, every movement or change of feature. Or, as chance might have it, he would lie farther away, to the side or rear, watching the outlines of the man and the occasional movements of his body. And often, such was the communion in which they lived, the strength of Buck's gaze would draw John Thornton's head around, and he would return the gaze, without speech, his heart shining out of his eyes as Buck's heart shone out."

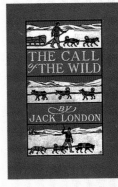

—Jack London, *The Call of the Wild*

280 *Cujo*

Stephen King's terrifying tale of a Saint Bernard gone mad from rabies. Also a terrifying film.

281 White Fang

Jack London's half-wolf, half-dog character from his 1906 follow-up book to *The Call of the Wild*. The story mirrors the first book in reverse, following the story of the wolf-dog who becomes civilized and is adopted into the world of man. London's writing style affords us an interesting look at how animals view the world.

282 *The Last Will and Testament of an Extremely Distinguished Dog*

Playwright Eugene O'Neill shares the pain of losing a special dog in an elegy written in the 1940s about his Dalmatian Silverdene Emblem O'Neill, known as Blemie. It is written in the voice of Blemie, and it eases the pain with reminders of the happiness they shared together.

283 Snoopy

Born at the Daisy Hill Puppy Farm, Snoopy, Charlie Brown's famous

"I WOULD LIKE TO BELIEVE THAT THERE IS A PARADISE. *Where one is always young and full-bladdered. Where all day one dillies and dallies. Where each blissful hour is mealtime. Where in long evenings there are a million fireplaces with logs forever burning, and one curls oneself up and blinks into the flames and nods and dreams, remembering the old brave days on earth and the love of one's Master and Mistress."*

—*Blemie O'Neill*, The Last Will and Testament of an Extremely Distinguished Dog

Beagle created by artist Charles Schulz, first appeared in the *Peanuts* cartoon strip on October 4, 1950, two days after the strip premiered. Over the 50 years that *Peanuts* ran in newspapers, Snoopy explored his alter egos. Sitting atop his doghouse, he became a World War I flying ace battling the Red Baron, as well as Joe Cool and a passionate writer who always began his stories with "It was a dark and stormy night. . . ." He was there at the finish, on January 3, 2000, to write the closing letter when *Peanuts* came to an end.

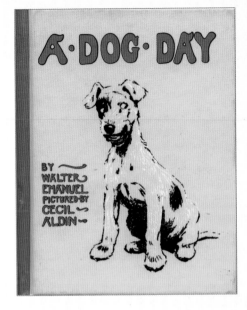

284 *Hank the Cowdog*

Hank is head of ranch security in the popular children's books written by John Erickson. Hank describes himself as "good old easy-going Hank who works hard, tries to do his job, and gets very little cooperation from anyone else around here." The illustrated adventures of *Hank the Cowdog* have become an integral part of school reading programs creating thousands of young devoted fans.

285 *A Dog Day*

A small book first published in 1902, *A Dog Day* is the story of a day in the life of a lovable pup told by the dog himself. In journal format, he writes, "9:40- While a visitor was being let in at the front door I rushed out, and had the most glorious roll in the mud. Felt more like my old self then. 10 to 10:15- Wagged tail." With illustrations by Cecil Aldin, this charming book by Walter Emanuel has been reprinted 20 times.

286 "Lassie Come Home"

While in Hollywood, Eric Knight acquired a Collie named Toots, who became the inspiration for the best seller "Lassie Come Home." Eric visited the set of the movie in 1942 but never lived to see the finished product. An army major, he was killed in action in World War II in 1943.

287 *Because of Winn-Dixie*

In Kate DiCamillo's novel, ten-year-old Opal befriends a big, funny dog and names him Winn-Dixie after the grocery store where she found him. Because of Winn-Dixie, she meets a cast of unforgettable characters and learns about friendship and acceptance.

288 The Dog Lovers Mysteries

Susan Conant's main character, amateur sleuth Holly Winter, along with her Alaskan Malamutes Kimi and Rowdy, solve murders in the secret world of dog shows, training clubs, and kennels. The Dog Lovers Mysteries include *The Wicked Flea, Stud Rights, Ruffly Speaking,* and *New Leash on Death.*

289 *The Angel by My Side*

Written by Mike Lingenfelter and David Frei, this true story tells of the life-altering devotion of Dakota, a Golden Retriever, who rescued Mike Ligenfelter from depression and heart disease. As the story unfolds, it is Mike who saves Dakota from life-threatening cancer.

290 *My Dog Skip*

Willie Morris tells the story of growing up with Skip, a Smooth Fox Terrier, in a sleepy Mississippi town. Skip amazed the locals by playing football and driving a car. This memoir of the deep love between an only child and his dog has touched the hearts of millions.

"I came across a photograph of him not long ago, his black face with the long snout sniffing at something in the air, his tail straight and pointing, his eyes flashing in some momentary excitement. Looking at a faded photograph taken more than forty years before, even as a grown man, I would admit I still missed him."

—Willie Morris, *My Dog Skip*

291
James Thurber

Humorist James Thurber had a lifelong love affair with dogs. His famous "Thurber hound" was a breed unto itself, appearing in countless *New Yorker* magazine cartoons and throughout his books. Thurber wrote about Poodles, Airedales, Scottish Terriers, Bloodhounds, German Shepherds, and Pugs. One of his most famous stories, "The Dog Who Bit People," involves an Airedale named Muggs. Thurber writes, "Mother used to send a box of candy every Christmas to the people the Airedale bit. The list finally contained forty or more names." In 1955, Simon and Schuster published the wonderful book *Thurber's Dogs: A Collection of the Master's Dogs, Written and Drawn, Real and Imaginary, Living and Long Ago.*

James Thurber with Christabel

thurber's dogs

A COLLECTION OF THE MASTER'S DOGS, WRITTEN AND DRAWN, REAL AND IMAGINARY, LIVING AND LONG AGO

JAMES THURBER

Terhune surrounded by his
beloved Collies.

Anice & Wolf. The trophies on the
bookshelf can be seen at the Van
Riper-Hopper House in New Jersey.

Lad (lying down), Bruce (sitting), Wolf (standing), and The Master

The Master at work.

"He was a big and incredibly powerful Collie, with a massive coat of burnished mahogany-and-snow and with absurdly small forepaws (which he spent at least an hour a day in washing) and with deepset dark eyes that seemed to have a soul behind them. So much for the outer dog. For the inner: he had a heart that did not know the meaning of fear or disloyalty or of meanness."

Albert Payson Terhune

It was his love for Lad that led Albert Payson Terhune to become a famous novelist at the age of 47 with the publication of *Lad: A Dog*. Those who read Terhune's books as children still have vivid memories of Lad: "Lad was an eighty-pound collie, thoroughbred in spirit as well as in build. . . . His shaggy coat, set off by the snowy ruff and chest, was like orange-flecked mahogany. His absurdly tiny forepaws, in which he took inordinate pride, were silver white."

Lad was bred to Lady, and produced a single surviving puppy, named Wolf. With this breeding, the Sunnybank Collies began their journey into the hearts and minds of a generation. Terhune would go on to write more than sixty books about his dogs and "The Place," also known as Sunnybank.

The story of Terhune would be incomplete without the story of Sunnybank, the estate built by his father and described in detail in the books. The lake, the sound of the Collies barking, the peaceful summer afternoons, and his life combined in a story of love for his dogs, his wife, Anice, and his family. These images permeate his writings and bring the dogs to life.

the modern dog culture magazine

THE

BARK

Dog is my co-pilot™

Smiling
Dogs
Galore!

Do Dogs Have a Funny Bone?

GEAR
**Up for Outdoor
Adventure**

TUNE IN:
**The Meaning
of Barking**

Step Out:
**2,200 Mile
Eco Trek**

A Guide to
Vet Advice;
**+Fixing
Bad
Knees**

Mo Rocca,
David Sedaris,
Merrill Markoe
think so.

**Our
Special
Humor
Issue**

Dog Crazed?
TAKE THE TEST

SUMMER 2005/# 31
$4.95US $6.9

293
The Bark

Oprah says it's a "must read." *Time* called it the *New Yorker* of dog magazines. From its simple beginnings as a newsletter back in 1997, *The Bark* has grown into a full-color publication for the new "dog culture." With articles by respected writers such as Erica Jong, Ann Patchett, David Sedaris, Merrill Markoe, and Alice Walker, it is a treasure for today's dog lover. Founders and partners Claudia Kawczynska and Cameron Woo have created a magazine that is beautifully designed, sophisticated, informative, and full of heart. Following the success of *The Bark*, Kawczynska and Woo put together *Dog is My Co-Pilot,* an anthology of great dog writing that became a *New York Times* best seller.

In the Spotlight

Countless clever and highly trained dogs have
entertained us at the movies and on TV.

294 Toto

Born in Altadena, California, in 1933, this adorable Cairn
Terrier (whose real name was Terry) was raised by Carl Spitz,
famed dog trainer to the stars. Although Terry began
her film career in 1934 in the movie *Bright Eyes*,
opposite Shirley Temple, she is most remembered
for her role as Toto in *The Wizard of Oz*. Terry
officially changed her name to Toto and went on
to make several more films, including *The Women*
(1939), with Joan Crawford and Norma Shearer.
Perhaps her lowest Hollywood moment was when, in a burst of
enthusiasm, she jumped from her crate to greet Clark Gable
and knocked his false teeth to the floor. She lives on in her
autobiography, *I, Toto*, by Willard Carroll and Linda Sunshine.

ABOVE: *With fellow cast members.*
RIGHT: *Setting out for a 1942 tour with
Carl Spitz's Hollywood Dog Stars. As
Toto says in her book, "I was a seasoned
professional by then and knew how to
find the lens."*

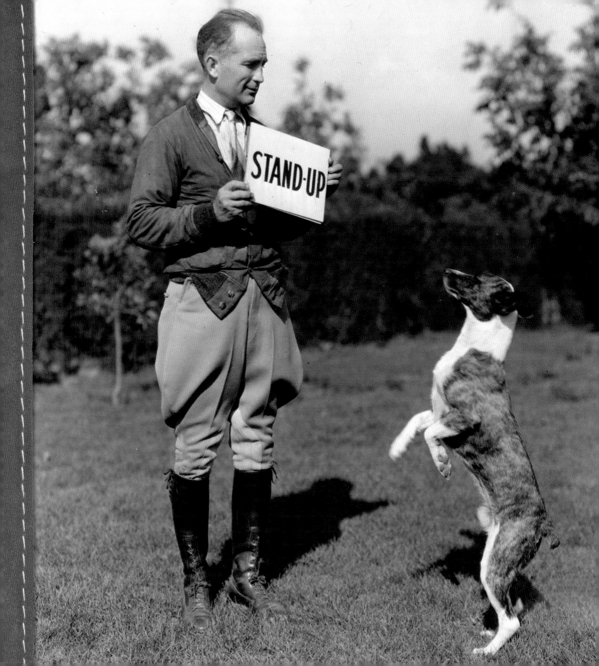

295
The stars of Dogville

In 1929, MGM began a series of comedy shorts called "Barkies," starring dog actors in clothing and featuring human voice-over dialogue and plots lifted from current MGM films of the day. The shorts employed numerous dogs taught by movie dog trainer Rennie Renfro.

Three stars stood out from the crowd. Jiggs, a mixed breed with pointy ears, was the character actor who played villains, detectives, and rascals. Buster was the leading-man type. And Oscar, the endearing Boston Terrier, played the female roles.

The films included *Hot Dog, College Hounds, The Dogville Murder Case, The Big Dog House,* and *Dogway Melody,* a parody of the 1929 musical *Broadway Melody.*

Until the series ended in 1931, the stars of the Dogville films had their own dressing rooms with air-conditioning and hot water.

OPPOSITE: *Rennie Renfro works with Buster.* LEFT: *Mrs. Renfro teaches a new trick to Oscar.*

296
Strongheart

The German Shepherd Strongheart, a major star of silent films, was discovered in Germany in 1920 and brought to Hollywood. Originally trained as an attack dog, he took to acting easily and became a wildly popular star after his first movie, *The Silent Call* (1921).

He appeared in several films and was often paired with Lady Jule, a female German Shepherd with whom he had a romance offscreen, siring many pups. In 1929, while on a movie set, Strongheart slipped and fell against a hot studio light, and he died of his injuries. J. Allen Boone wrote the wonderful book *Kinship with All Life* based on his experience with Strongheart.

"From coast to coast, newspapers, magazines, the radio and electric signs were proclaiming to the world that a sensational new star had appeared in the movie heavens, that he was a dog and that his name was Strongheart."

—J. Allen Boone, *Kinship with All Life*

STRONGHEART

297
Rin Tin Tin

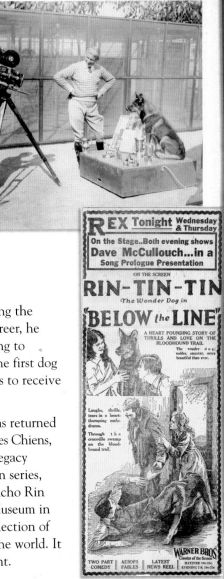

The original Rin Tin Tin was a German Shepherd puppy found by American serviceman Lee Duncan in a bombed-out war dog kennel in Lorraine, France, just before the end of World War I. Named for a French puppet, Rin Tin Tin accompanied Duncan back to California at the end of the war. It was in Los Angeles that the dog was discovered by producer Darryl F. Zanuck while performing at a dog show. (He could jump 13.5 feet over obstacles!)

Rin Tin Tin began his film career playing a wolf, and he went on to appear in 26 films, one of which was such a success that he was credited with saving the Warner Brothers studio from bankruptcy. At the peak of his career, he dined on steak prepared by his own personal chef while listening to classical music. Rin Tin Tin had his own radio show and was the first dog in history to ride in a plane. And he was one of only three dogs to receive a star on the Hollywood Walk of Fame.

Upon his death in 1932, Rin Tin Tin was returned to France to be buried in the Cimetière des Chiens, the famous pet cemetery in Paris. His legacy continued in a popular 1950s television series, and his lineage is carried on at El Rancho Rin Tin Tin in Texas. The Rin Tin Tin Museum in Latexo, Texas, houses the largest collection of German Shepherd memorabilia in the world. It is open to the public by appointment.

111

298 Asta

A Frank Weatherwax protégé, Asta (whose real name was Skippy) starred in the 1934 screwball comedy *The Thin Man*, with William Powell and Myrna Loy as Nick and Nora Charles. Ace detective Nick investigated crimes and Nora aided him while mixing martinis in Art Deco hotel rooms, but it was Asta who stole the show, cornering suspects and unearthing crucial evidence.

This lovable Wire Fox Terrier was extremely popular and helped promote the breed. In the original novel by Dashiell Hammett, Asta was a Schnauzer.

Skippy's other film credits include *Bringing Up Baby*, with Katharine Hepburn, and *Topper Takes a Trip*.

299 *Lady and the Tramp*

Disney's classic 1955 love story between a street-smart mongrel and a sophisticated purebred Cocker Spaniel. Most memorable moment: eating spaghetti at an Italian restaurant.

300 *101 Dalmatians*

The 1961 animated film brought us Cruella De Vil and 15 adorable Dalmatian puppies.

301 *Old Yeller*

Disney produced this classic dog movie, based on the book by Fred Gipson, in 1957. The story takes place just after the Civil War and explores the relationship between a struggling Texas family and the big dog who comes into their lives unannounced. The role of Old Yeller was played by Spike, a large yellow dog with huge feet and floppy ears. Frank Weatherwax rescued him from a Van Nuys, California, animal shelter for $3 and trained him for the part. Spike continued his career in film and television, and he ultimately passed on his acting talent to his grandson, who played opposite Steve McQueen in the 1972 film *Junior Bonner*.

302 Brutus

Brutus was an invisible German Shepherd who kills the title character in the 1944 film *The Invisible Man's Revenge*.

"We called him Old Yeller. The name had a sort of double meaning. One part meant that his short hair was a dingy yellow, a color that we called "yeller" in those days. The other meant that when he opened his head, the sound he let out came closer to being a yell than a bark."

—Fred Gipson, *Old Yeller*, 1956

303 The dogs of Harry Potter

Fang, Hagrid's "boarhound," was played in the first film by four different Neapolitan Mastiffs. Bully, one of the four, had been rescued from a junkyard. With computer help, Fluffy played the three-headed dog guarding the door to the chamber that held the Sorcerer's Stone. Fluffy was based on Cerberus, the dog in Greek mythology that guards the gates of the underworld. As with Cerberus, Fluffy could be subdued and lulled to sleep only by music.

304 Beethoven

The popular movie serie
tells the tale of a Saint
Bernard puppy who ado
a family and changes th
lives of everyone.

305 Boots

Boots, the sickly runt of
litter of pups, was adopt
by animal trainer Bert
Rose. Because of Rose's
nurturing, training, and
love, Boots survived and
came to display "star
quality." Boots could
understand over 800
words and follow verbal
instructions on the mov
sets. He ultimately made
more than a dozen films
and during World War I
he traveled with the US
entertaining the troops.
He is credited with sellir
$9 million worth of war
bonds.

306 Benji

Discovered in a Burbank, California, shelter by animal trainer Frank Inn, Benji (whose real name was Higgins) began his acting career on the television show *Petticoat Junction* in the 1960s. Higgins was an adorable Poodle, Cocker Spaniel, and Schnauzer mix with an expressive face and the ability to learn clever tricks, including yawning and sneezing on cue.

He found success on the silver screen, debuting in the movie *Benji* in 1974. Higgins (and his progeny) made a series of popular movies and television shows, with revenues from movies, TV, books, and products topping $235 million.

Over 73 million people have gone to see Benji at the movies, and over one billion people worldwide have watched Benji on television. Benji was honored by being the second animal to be inducted into the Animal Actors Hall of Fame, preceded only by Lassie. Perhaps his greatest contribution was to homeless pets. According to the American Humane Association, because the original Benji was rescued from a shelter, more than 1 million dogs have been adopted from shelters across America.

307
Lassie

Lassie began her amazing life as a character in "Lassie Come Home," a 1938 short story by author Eric Knight. Later expanded into a novel, the story was also made into a movie in 1943, starring Roddy McDowall and Elizabeth Taylor. The first dog to play Lassie in movies was a Collie named Pal, owned by animal trainer Rudd Weatherwax and his brother Frank. All the dogs who played Lassie were male, due to their thicker coats. The eighth Lassie appeared in the 1994 film *Lassie, Best Friends Are Forever*. Lassie's popularity continued

through her successful 19-year run on television, portraying the amazing, super-intelligent dog who could understand everything Timmy had to say, especially when there was quicksand involved or she needed to go get Doc Weaver. The Weatherwax family continues to breed and train Collies to this day.

308 Cleo, the Basset Hound on *The People's Choice*

Played by Bernadette, Cleo starred in the popular late 1950s sitcom *The People's Choice*, opposite Jackie Cooper. This long-eared, thoughtful Basset Hound always had something on her mind when it came to her hapless human companions, and only the audience could hear what she had to say (with the voice-over courtesy of Mary Jane Croft). Originally purchased for $84, Bernadette was trained by Frank Inn, and she went on to win the coveted PATSY award (Picture Animals Top Star of the Year) in 1958.

309 Never fear! Underdog is here!

The Superman of Dogdom, Underdog was always there to save the day when his girlfriend, Sweet Polly Purebred, was in a predicament. His alter ego, mild-mannered Shoeshine Boy, would find a phone booth and slip into his superhero costume. The show's beginning echoed its human counterpart's famous phrase: "Look, up in the sky, it's a bird, it's a plane, it's a frog . . . a frog?" "Not bird, nor plane, nor even frog, it's just little ol' me, Underdog!"

310 Mr. Peabody

Set the WABAC Machine for 1959! Mr. Hector Peabody, scientist, inventor, Harvard graduate, and small white dog, debuted in 1959 in "Peabody's Improbable History," costarring his pet boy, Sherman. Peabody, a genius of sorts, and Sherman explored history with the help of their time machine and got involved in famous events, always making sure they came out right.

311 Our all-time favorite cartoon dogs

Huckleberry Hound, Deputy Dawg, Manfred the Mighty Wonder Dog, Augie Doggie and Doggie Daddy, Goofy, Pluto, Scooby Doo, Astro (*The Jetsons*), Clifford the Big Red Dog, Dino (*The Flintstones*), Dogbert (dog of Dilbert), Sandy (who belonged to Little Orphan Annie), Gromit (associate of Wallace), and Buster Brown's Tige.

Moose was spokesdog for a Celebrity Pro-Am golf tournament in 2003.

312
Eddie, from
NBC's *Frasier*

Eddie, the popular Jack Russell Terrier
played by Moose, appeared on the
sitcom *Frasier* from 1993 to 2004.
Costar David Hyde Pierce called him
"Laurence Olivier in a hair shirt."

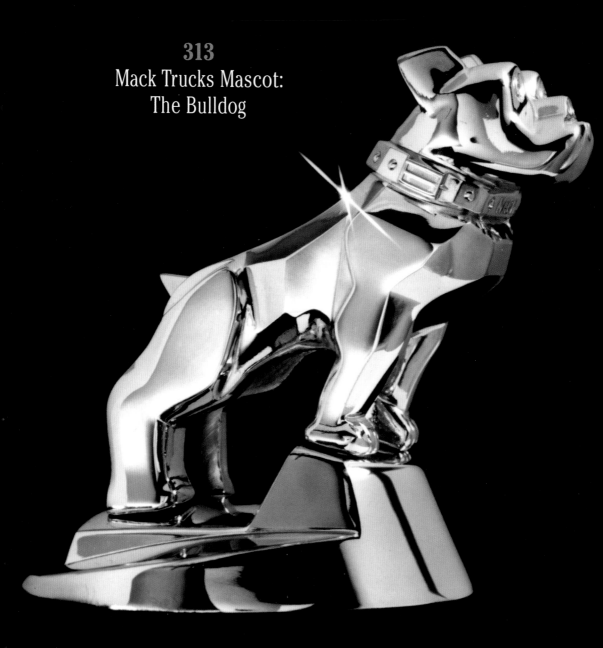

313
Mack Trucks Mascot:
The Bulldog

314 Farfel

Spokesdog for Nestle's Quik from 1953 to 1965, Farfel appeared with ventriloquist Jimmy Nelson as a regular on *The Ed Sullivan Show*.

315 Spuds Mackenzie

Mascot for Bud Light beer from 1987 to 1989, this white Bull Terrier was billed as the "Ultimate Party Animal." In real life, Spuds was a female named Honey Tree Evil Eye.

316 Nipper

Nipper, who became one of the most famous trademarks of modern times, was born in Bristol in 1884. When his first owner died, Nipper was taken to live with artist Francis Barraud, the first owner's younger brother. Barraud captured Nipper's attentive expression and tilted head as the dog listened to "His Master's Voice." The image was patented in 1900 and ultimately became famous as the symbol of RCA Victor.

317 The Hush Puppy dog

Jason, a Basset Hound, became the face of Hush Puppies in the late 1980s in a series of clever ads by the Fallon McElligott agency.

You Ain't Nothin' But a Hound Dog

And other canine moments in the history of music.

318 Elegy on the Death of a Poodle
Beethoven composed this music in 1787 in memory of a dear Poodle. The lyrics from an unknown author reflect on the thoughts that everything we love is only borrowed, and that the dog will live on in happy memories.

319 La Valse du Petit Chien
Chopin composed this piece, better known as "The Minute Waltz," in 1847, inspired by the antics of a Poodle that belonged to author George Sand.

320 Chihuahua Waltz
Written and performed by guitarist John Knowles.

321 How Much Is That Doggie in the Window?
The one with the waggly tail was a chart-topping success for Patti Page in 1953.

322 Walkin' the Dog
Recorded by Rufus Thomas. If you don't know the way to do it, he'll show you how to walk the dog.

323 Me and You and a Dog Named Boo
A hit for Lobo in 1971.

324 Oh Where, Oh Where Has My Little Dog Gone?
Written by Septimus Winner during the Civil War, the melody is from a German folk song called "Lauterbach."

325 Martha My Dear
This Lennon and McCartney hit first appeared on the "White Album" in 1968. While many believe that it was written for his sheepdog, Martha, McCartney claims the dog was named for his muse, Martha, who is the real subject of the song.

326 Hound Dog
A song by Lieber and Stoller, it was first recorded by Big Mama Thornton in 1953, followed by Elvis Presley in 1956. Still a classic.

327 Who Let the Dogs Out?
A huge hit for the Baha Men in 2000, it became a popular sports anthem around the world.

328
B-I-N-G-O . . . B-I-N-G-O . . . B-I-N-G-O
And Bingo was his name-o!

Party Animals

"The greatest pleasure of a dog is that you may make a fool of yourself with him, and not only will he not scold you, but he will make a fool of himself too."

—Samuel Butler

Simple Pleasures

Dogs find great joy in the simplest things in life, and share their happiness with us in so many ways.

329 The first stretch of the morning

330 Inhaling your food

331 Resting under a shade tree in the heat of the summer

332 Company!!!

333 A playdate

334 The joys of rolling in all things odoriferous

335 A little nap after a morning walk

336 Dinnertime

337 Sleeping by the fire

338 The amble

339 Barking for joy

340 Rubbing your back in the grass

341 Going for a swim on a hot day

342 Sunbathing

343
An afternoon snooze
on forbidden furniture
when no one
is home

344
Running full tilt in figure eights

345
Walkie time

357
Grabbing a little
snack between meals

359
Fillet of sole

358
Helping make lunch

360
Being invited to a barbecue

361
The smell of bacon
first thing in the
morning

"He had as much fun in the water as any person I have known. You didn't have to throw a stick in the water to get him to go in. Of course, he would bring back a stick to you if you did throw one in. He would even have brought back a piano if you had thrown one in."

—James Thurber

362
A grand leap into
the water

363
Sitting on laps

374
Frisbees!

375
Tennis balls!

376
Getting your person to
throw the ball just
one more time

377
Learning
new tricks

"Number one way life would be
different if dogs ran the world:
All motorists must drive with
head out window."

—David Letterman

378 Being a foot warmer

379 Scratching

380 Enthusiastic, tail-wagging
greetings at the door

381 Swimming just for the joy of swimming

382 Watching out the window for
approaching squirrels

383 A big yawn before settling into an
afternoon sleep

384 The lightness of step on the first cool
day of autumn

385 A brisk walk in a forest filled with wild
scents

386 Marking one's territory

387 Chasing anything

388 The smell of being freshly bathed

389 Barking at the doorbell, even if it's on TV

390
Going places in
the car

391
A really big
shake after
a bath

392
Knowing you look
fabulous right after
a grooming

393
Sleeping under the covers

394
The scent of a
forgotten biscuit
in a pocket

395
The sound of the
refrigerator
opening

396 Watching the world from YOUR spot by the window

397 Willingly providing a rinse cycle before plates go in the dishwasher

398 Cleaning up scraps that fall on the kitchen floor

399 Digging for digging's sake

400 Your first Christmas

401 The bone dance

402 Unwrapping a birthday present, and shredding the paper

403 Providing "homeland security" with a bark in the middle of the night

404 Hearing the word "walk" (even if they spell it)

405 The sound of YOUR car in the driveway

406 Carrying dirty socks

407 Fetching . . . sometimes

408 The zen of chasing one's tail

409 Dragging a leash to the door

410 Baying at the full moon

411 Dashing through the snow

412 Harmonizing with the neighbor's dog

413 A sweet hug from a little child

414 Almost catching a squirrel

415 Cat food

416 Milk-Bones, marrow bones, any bones!

417 A new squeaky toy

418 The moment of sweet forgiveness after a reprimand

419 The secret rhythm of each day

420
Someone to love you
and tell you're
wonderful

The Pampered Pooch

When nothing but the best will do, there are many ways to indulge our favorite dogs. Gourmet meals, herbal treatments, a custom doghouse, and plenty of bling!

421 **A weekend at the Ritz**

At the Ritz Canine Spa in Worcester, England, dogs swim in a heated indoor pool with underwater jets. After a swim session, they are given heated towels and homemade cookies. Dog massage and acupuncture are provided in the Zen Den. And there is a professional photographer on-site to record all the pampering.

422 **Escaping to Bangkok's Indo-Thai Dog Resort and Spa**

Lucky dogs enjoy herbal treatments, a swim in the exercise pool, Ayurvedic powder rubs, hot-stone therapies, a soak in a petal-strewn, orange-scented tub, and three healthy meals.

423 **Becoming a regular at Camp Canine Country Club and Spa in Boca Raton, Florida**

Dogs cavort in the cageless indoor playgrounds and venture outside (in cooler weather) for a romp on the jungle gyms in the fenced-in outdoor play area. Camp Canine offers day care, boarding, training, grooming, snack time, and nap time. It even has rainy-day doggie movies!

424 **Biscuits & Bath**

A country club for dogs in the heart of New York, Biscuits & Bath offers services such as training, day care, play groups for small dogs, and grooming.

425

Having your own personal photographer who knows how to make you look fabulous

*Fredrik and Mondrian,
photographed by Sue Akin
and Donald Fowler,
akin-fowler.com*

426 An enchanted evening at the Ritzy Canine Carriage House, New York

This Midtown Manhattan luxury dog facility offers gourmet cuisine prepared by the in-house chef, room service, a private presidential suite, exercise in its outdoor skytop playroom, both day and overnight care, and nightly turndown service.

427 A private room at the kennel playing your favorite TV programs

428 A cottage with a porch in the dog run

429 An edible Crunchkins greeting card from your dog's play pal

430 An Anxiety Wrap for life's stressful moments

The Anxiety Wrap is a holistic approach to behavior modification increasing body awareness and relieving stress, tension, and anxieties.

431 Staying cool with a Canine Icer wrap for sore muscles

432 Having your own veterinary canine chiropractor

433 A Legally Pink town house for your Legally Blonde Chihuahua

434 Swim therapy sessions at Pamplin Animal Wellness Services (PAWS) in Virginia, under the expert guidance of Dr. Regina Schwabe

435 A fabulous Eloise bed

The Vicki Wagner–designed pillow beds grace many celebrity homes and Starwood Hotels' pet-friendly rooms.

436 Sleeping like royalty in an Imperial Crown bed, perfect for the czar or czarina of the house

437 A Louis Vuitton Sac Chien: $2,250

438 A Swarovski Crystal collar

439 An 8-inch, 6-carat diamond collar: only $7,500

440 Dog bling

441
Shopping online for the perfect gift for that special someone at thegildedpaw.com

When only the very best is good enough for your dog, visit thegildedpaw.com online and browse its fabulous selection of beds and furniture, dog apparel, designer pet carriers, toys, dinnerware, and accessories. Its also stocks the basics in terms of collars, leads, and harnesses.

"A thing of beauty is a joy forever."
—John Keats

The Gilded Paw
Distinctive Products for Dogs & Cats

151

453 Chiengora
Similar in look and feel to the soft and fluffy angora yarns, Chiengora is created by spinning hair collected from your favorite dog. It can be knitted into hats, scarves, mittens, and sweaters. Chiengora fluffs as it's worn and is water-resistant. Best of all, when spun correctly, it doesn't shed!

454 A $300 hair dryer

455 Swarovski Collar Charms

456 A collar tag in your zodiac gemstone

457 Pink sapphire Swarovski Crystal ID tags with a matching collar

458 A Bone-a-Fido couch in olive plaid, with the signature dog-bone end pieces

459 A Bolduc custom hand-tooled bridle leather leash

460 A braided Kangaroo leather designer show lead

461 A Comfort Heartbeat pillow for the new puppy

462
The Jackie O. Pink Pill Box Hat

463
Finding the perfect dress to wear to Mommy's wedding

153

Distinctive Products for Dogs & Cats

464
Jimmy Chews,
Dog Perignon, and
a Hairy Winston
wedding ring

465
A wedding in
Vegas

466 Soft Posh Pearl necklace
No more nagging neck pain from
sleeping on rock-hard jewels!

467 Personalized postage
stamps with your
dog's picture from
photostamps.com

468 A custom-designed pet
armoire from the Bark
Avenue Pet Boutique on
Amelia Island, Florida

469
A place to rest your
weary bones

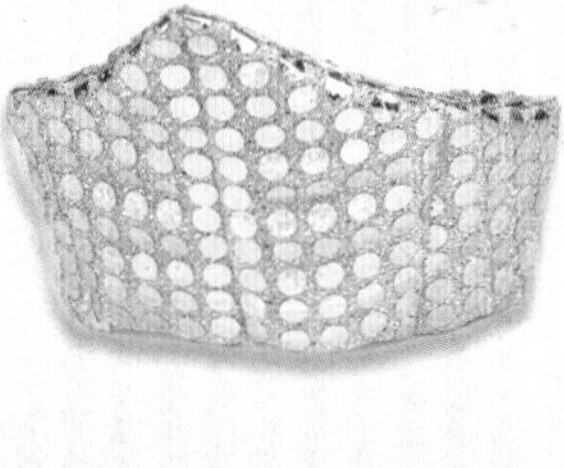

470 A Dog Dreams CD
Created by composer
Marco Missinato and
Brandon Fouche,
an expert in canine
communication, this
CD offers a selection
of soft melodies
intended to calm
and balance your
dog. Songs include
"A Ball to Catch,"
"Thumping Tail,"
"Nudging for
Cuddles," and "We'll
Never Say Goodbye."

471 The Dog Sitter DVD
Watch squirrels, raccoons, cats, and more from the comfort
of your own couch. Produced with enhanced sound
for dogs, this video includes subliminal
messages that say, "Good dog, good dog!"

*Canine models Gigi, Sir Byron, and Anakin
from The Gilded Paw*

happytails
Canine Spa Line

Indulging in the products from the Happytails Canine Spa Line

Happytails Canine Spa Line takes canine pampering to a whole new level. Its natural dog shampoos contain the finest botanical and herbal extracts, while its holistic products are used in canine massage and aromatherapy.

The line includes products with names like Dog Smog Remedy (a breath freshener and digestive solution that curtails emissions from both ends) and Flea the Scene (an insect spray with sunscreen). For a subtle hint of glitter to the coat, try its Sparkle & Shine Shimmering Mist, which not only looks fabulous but helps repel dirt!

It even has gift packs for the Spa Dog, the Metro Dog, and the Celebrity Dog.

But best of all, a portion of the profits is donated to Canine Companions for Independence, a nonprofit organization that provides highly trained assistance dogs to people with disabilities.

473
A room with
a view

474
Barkitecture:
the new doghouse

Designers and architects are
creating some amazing homes
for today's lucky dogs.

475
The Doghouse-
Birdhouse-Lighthouse

Designed by Susan Dinion of Roberts
Dinion Architects of Massachusetts
and built by Ken Vona, this seaside
doghouse (which also featured a birdhouse)
started a bidding war at a charity auction. It ultimately raised $8,000 for the
Hull Seaside Animal Rescue. According to the program, "This distinctive
seashore home features spacious quarters in which to lounge after a difficult
day of chasing cats. A stunning 5-foot-high authentic lighthouse creates
a landmark in the neighborhood with working rotating light and
observation deck. . . . This cozy canine cottage is the ideal
retreat for dog-day afternoons." Its creators followed their
success with Fenway Bark, a replica of Boston's famous
baseball stadium.

161

Going to the Dogs

Dog lovers can find endless places to explore
and discover the world of dogs.

476 The American Kennel Club Museum of the Dog, St. Louis

The historic Monsanto Jarville House, an 1853 Greek Revival mansion in Queeny Park, in St. Louis, is the perfect location to highlight the museum's fine and varied collections.

In 1971, the Westminster Kennel Club established a foundation to gather and collect knowledge on the care, history, and heritage of the dog in America. In conjunction with the American Kennel Club, the Dog Museum was formed and, under the direction of William Secord, had its first exhibit on February 8, 1982.

The museum publishes a newsletter, *Sirius*, which has information on exhibitions, acquisitions, and upcoming events.

OPPOSITE: Willpower (Sweet Temptation) by Charles van den Eycken, 1891. From the collection of the American Kennel Club Museum of the Dog

477 Making a pilgrimage to the Saint Bernard Monastery, home of the famous rescue dogs

In 962, Saint Bernard founded a monastery and hospice for the protection of travelers, at the highest point of the dangerous mountain pass between Aosta in Italy and the Valais in Switzerland. It is here that the Saint Bernard breed developed and flourished, saving over 2,000 people during the 200 years that the dogs served at the monastery.

163

An afternoon of research at
The American Kennel Club Library

Located in New York City, the library is open to the public a
currently contains over 17,000 volumes, including stud book
art, literature, history, and sporting books. In addition,
there are many outstanding pieces of art, including
paintings and ceramics, on display
throughout the library.

479 The National Bird Dog Museum, Field Trial Hall of Fame, & Wildlife Heritage Center

This relatively new museum, located 50 miles east of Memphis in Grand Junction, preserves the past and protects the future of the sporting dog breeds in America. It is a mixture of art, information, photography, and memorabilia about bird dogs. The Retriever Hall of Fame honors those dogs demonstrating excellence in retrieving, obedience, companionship, and service to hunters.

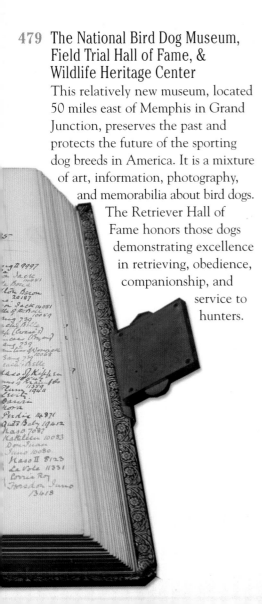

480 Pebble Hill Plantation

This 1820s Greek Revival home located in Thomasville, Georgia, is furnished with art, antiques, porcelains, crystal, silver, and Native American relics belonging to the Hanna family of Ohio. The art collection includes 19th-century dog paintings by John Emms, Maud Earl, and Arthur Wardle.

481 El Rancho Rin Tin Tin

One of the world's largest collections of German Shepherd Dog memorabilia, the Rin Tin Tin museum has more than 8,000 pieces of rare and unusual collectibles, including porcelains, lobby cards, books, plush toys, pictures, puzzles and games, comics, magazines, and posters. Open to the public by appointment, it is located midway between Houston and Dallas in Latexo, Texas. An added bonus: visitors can meet the descendants of the original Rin Tin Tin at El Rancho Rin Tin Tin.

482

Spending a summer day at Sunnybank

Home to beloved author Albert Payson Terhune and his family of Collies, including the famous Lad from his popular book *Lad: A Dog*, Sunnybank has been protected and preserved through the efforts of a number of people, including Claire Leishman, a local resident who founded the Terhune Sunnybank Memorial Fund. Although the original house is no longer standing, one can visit the graves of the dogs in this beautiful setting, now known as Terhune Memorial Park. Today, Terhune Memorial Park, overlooking Wayne Township, New Jersey, is a living monument to the Terhunes and their Collies.

"I wonder if it is heretical to believe that when at last my tired feet shall tread the Other Shore, a madly welcoming swirl of exultant collies—the splendid Sunnybank dogs that have been my chums here—will bound forward, circling and barking around me, to lead me Home!"

—*Albert Payson Terhune*

483
The William Secord Gallery, New York

The William Secord Gallery specializes in the sale and exhibition of fine dog paintings, bronzes, and works on paper. William Secord is considered the world's leading authority on 19th-century dog painting. The works of Maud Earl, Sir Edwin Landseer, Alfred Duke, and Charles Olivier de Penne are featured along with modern artists such as Morgan Dennis, Christine Merrill, Constance Payne, and Charlotte Sorre.

ABOVE: English Pointers in a Landscape *by Thomas Blinks;* RIGHT: Seated Bichon Frise *by Christine Merrill;* OPPOSITE: *William Secord Gallery. Images courtesy William Secord Gallery, Inc., New York*

484 The Presidential Pet Museum

Just 19 miles from the White House, this museum, established in 1999, houses artifacts and items related to the first pets. Included in the collection is a portrait of Lucky, the Reagans' Bouvier des Flandres, made from her own hair. The Pet Museum is open to the public by appointment.

485 A weekend at a Loews Hotel

Loews Hotels feature special treatment for both pets and their owners. You will receive a personal note from the general manager with information on hotel pet services, local dog-walking routes, puppy pagers, and area pet services such as veterinarians, pet shops, groomers, and much more. Loews features a "Did You Forget Closet," which stocks leashes and collars, pet videos, and dog (and cat) beds.

486 Hartsdale Pet Cemetery

In 1896, New York veterinarian Samuel Johnson kindly offered a spot in his apple orchard to a friend whose beloved dog had passed away. The beautiful hillside orchard would become America's first pet cemetery, and eventually the final resting place for nearly 70,000 pets. Within the grounds, in Lothian, Maryland, one can find show dogs, Seeing Eye dogs, war dogs, dogs of celebrities, and beloved pets. Sirius, the only dog to lose his life during search and-rescue efforts following the terrorist attacks of 9/11, is buried here.

487 Staying at the Madison Hotel in Washington, D.C., just for the "Paw Paw" special, including an in-room doggie dining menu

488 Stopping at the Canine "Honor Bar" at the Hotel Vintage Plaza in Portland, Oregon, stocked with a supply of "Frosty Paws" ice cream

489 In the Raw dog bar, Scottsdale, Arizona

A coffee bar, juice bar, and dog lover's spot in Scottsdale, Arizona, In the Raw is all about dogs. Canine customers are invited to dine on the patio next to the fire hydrant drinking fountain.

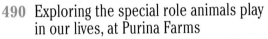

490 Exploring the special role animals play in our lives, at Purina Farms

Located in Gray Summit, Missouri, Purina Farms combines a tourist center and two competition areas. Visitors can learn about pets and pet nutrition and view dogs (and cats) at the Pet Center. There is an educational display on the history of Ralston Purina, and training demonstrations, dog agility demonstrations, and swimming are scheduled throughout the day. Videos of some of the major dog shows held at the farm are played, and experts are on hand to answer obedience training questions as well as provide grooming information. The grounds of Purina Farms serve as official show grounds for many dog clubs. Agility events, Terrier trials, lure coursing, and other events are open to the public.

172

497
Going to the Big Apple
Circus just to see the dogs

The Muttville Comix Troupe of Dogs

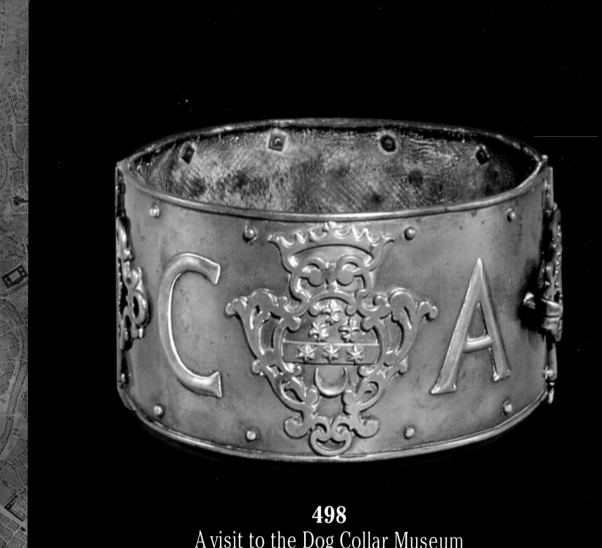

498
A visit to the Dog Collar Museum
in Leeds Castle, Kent, England

Leeds Castle is the site of a unique collection of historical dog collars. Lady Baillie, the American-born heiress to the Whitney fortune, purchased the castle in 1926. The Leeds Castle Foundation was created in 1974 to preserve and restore the castle.

Mrs. Gertrude Hunt presented the collection of dog collars to the foundation in memory of her husband, a noted medievalist. The collection includes over 100 collars, some dating back to the 15th and 16th centuries. During that time, the purpose of the dog collar was to protect the throat of the hunting dog against attacks from wolves, bears, and wild boars. These broad iron collars were adorned with spikes.

In later centuries, the function of the dog collar evolved to that of decoration and identification. The museum exhibit includes many examples of outstanding baroque leather and velvet collars. Engraved silver collars from the 19th century run from the very formal to the less so. One brass dog collar is engraved with this inscription: "I am Mr. Pratt's Dog, King St., Nr Wokingham, Berks. Whose Dog are You?"

175

499 Antiquibles

Barbara and David Hays have been collecting dog items since 1967. Add to that the collection of Julia Speegle Hall, who collected from the 1920s to the 1950s, and you have the amazing Antiquibles Dog Museum. The museum has over 8,000 different items related to dogs, with over 100 categories of collecting, such as bronze, iron, porcelain, glass, advertising, and art. The range of dogs is wide (from tiny depression-era celluloid toys to Meissen and fine oil paintings). Some of the more unusual dog items in the museum include a 1700s rifle with dog-head stock, an aluminum figural Scottie heater, a cast iron dog-head hitching post, an 1800s automaton Bulldog, a rare tin windup racing Greyhound toy, and a Victorian taxidermy Bulldog.

The museum has been the subject of a number of articles and television programs, including *An American Moment* with James Earl Jones. It is housed in the Antiquibles Mall, located four miles north of Waco, Texas.

176

00 Visiting the monument to Boatswain, Lord Byron's Newfoundland, in Newstead Abbey, Nottinghamshire, England

The inscription on the monument to Byron's beloved dog reads:

NEAR THIS SPOT
ARE DEPOSITED THE
REMAINS OF ONE
WHO POSSESSED BEAUTY
    WITHOUT VANITY,
STRENGTH WITHOUT INSOLENCE,
COURAGE WITHOUT FEROCITY,
AND ALL THE VIRTUES OF MAN
    WITHOUT HIS VICES.
THIS PRAISE, WHICH WOULD BE
    UNMEANING FLATTERY
IF INSCRIBED OVER HUMAN ASHES,
IS BUT A JUST TRIBUTE TO THE
MEMORY OF
BOATSWAIN, A DOG
WHO WAS BORN AT
    NEWFOUNDLAND, MAY, 1803,
AND DIED AT NEWSTEAD,
    NOV. 18TH, 1808.

501 Going to Guisachan

Guisachan, located just outside the village of Tomich in northern Scotland, is the birthplace of the Golden Retriever. The ruins of the original mansion, as well as the original kennel building, still remain. Lord Tweedmouth and his heirs lived on the estate while developing the Golden Retreiver breed in the mid-1800s. It is rumored that Winston Churchill learned to drive a car during his visits to the estate as a young boy.

There is a guest house in Tomich, owned by the Fraser family, that accepts visitors from March through November.

502 Le Cimetière des Chiens, Paris

During the 1800s, the role of animals in the lives of people changed dramatically from one of a utilitarian nature to that of companion and family member. Our attitude toward animals, and our treatment of them, changed as well. Beginning in 1824, the Society for the Protection of Animals was started in England, followed shortly by the SPA in France.

The Cimetière des Chiens was founded in the summer of 1899 to create a resting place for the beloved companions of the people of Paris. Located in Asnieres, northwest of Paris, on a quiet part of the Seine, the cemetery was created through the work of lawyer Georges Harmois and journalist Marguerite Durand.

At the grand entrance is a statue of Barry, the famous Saint Bernard. While canine luminaries such as Rin Tin Tin and police dogs of honor have found their resting place here, the majority are the beloved companions of regular people. Near the entrance to the cemetery is a plaque commemorating a stray dog who, in 1958, died at the gates of the cemetery and became the 40,000th animal to be buried within its walls. Dogs share this lovely spot with horses, cats, birds, and monkeys.

503 Stephen Huneck's Dog Chapel on Dog Mountain, St. Johnsbury, Vermont

Artist Stephen Huneck found his vision for Dog Chapel through a tragic accident. After suffering a fall in his home, Huneck developed Adult Respiratory Distress Syndrome and slipped into a two-month coma. To the surprise of his doctors, he survived and came home to learn to walk again. His dogs were always by his side, nudging him on and waiting patiently for him to catch up. Not long after returning home, he came up with the idea of building the chapel to celebrate the bond we have with our dogs. Begun in 1997, it now stands on Dog Mountain, Huneck's 400-acre mountaintop farm. Sunlight streams through stained-glass windows that tell of the lessons he learned from his dogs about the nature of love, joy, friendship, trust, faith, and peace. In his book *The Dog Chapel*, Huneck says, "You too can build a chapel in memory of your dog, in a place that is always open—your heart."

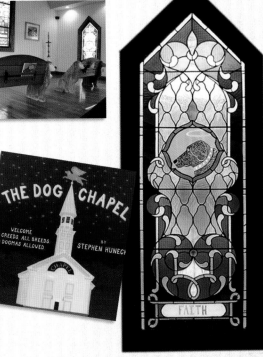

What's for Dinner?

A dog's favorite moment of the day!

504 The intense concentration of watching dinner being prepared

505 A pre-dinner dance

506 Being ready to pounce on anything that falls to the floor

507 Knowing the words "Do you want to eat," "dinnertime," and "dish"

508 The sound of water being slurped from the bowl

509 Catching a biscuit in midair

510 Drooling

511 Cleaning the bowl

512 Licking your littermate's face

513 Babies fumbling with cookies

514 Begging for biscuits

515 Sitting under the table hoping for a little tidbit from a kind person

516
Your very own
monogrammed
designer food and
water dish

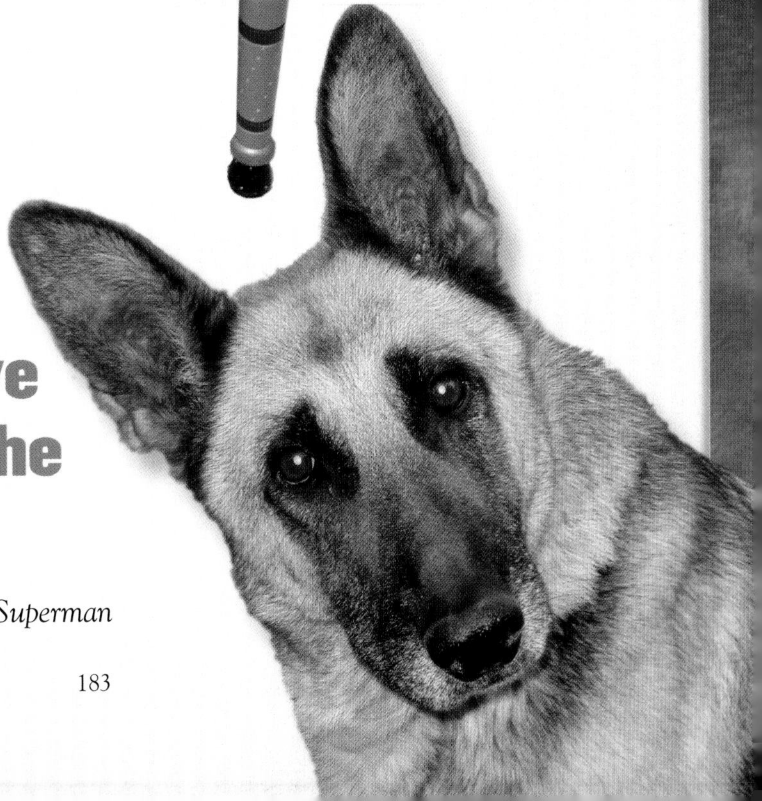

"There is no love sincerer than the love of food."

—George Bernard Shaw, *Man and Superman*

Keep your dog happy and fit on Rin Tin Tin's own balanced diet—**MILK-BONE** and **PAL TINY BITS**

HE KNOWS!

Table scraps do not satisfy the dog's need for balanced diet. Science has combined precious food values into one balanced food—Ken-L-Ration, famous for its supreme quality. Feed your dog Ken-L-Ration and watch him improve in health and appearance. It is U. S. Inspected ... as pure as the food served on your own table. Beware of unin-spected dog foods. Ken-L-Ration is for sale at quality stores.

CHAPPEL BROS., INC.
89 Peoples Ave. Rockford, Ill.

DOG
BIOGRAPHIES
FREE
Send a Ken-L-Ration label
for a Free Copy

KEN-L-RATION
THE DOG FOOD SUPREME

517

The classics
of dog food:
Friskies,
Red Heart,
Pard, Dash, Cadillac,
Ken-L-Ration,
Gravy Train, Alpo,
Gaines Burgers

As good as it looks...
it's the same fine **PARD!**

This is PARD before Dehydration

This is PARD dehydrated water added-ready to serve

Pard dehydration is entirely different!

Fires up energy ...Friskies!

Full nourishment that rings the bell! Four-alarm flavor that sparks the fussiest appetite! That's Friskies. Every serving gives your dog all the vitamins, minerals and protein a dog is known to need. Plus meaty-rich flavor and aroma that bring dogs racing to the scene! No wonder Friskies is the chief of all quality brand dog foods. Step your dog up the ladder to Friskies. It's another quality pet food from *Carnation*

Friskies
DOG FOOD

HE'S A
Friskies Fed
CHAMPION

RECORD ...

Keep your dogs frisky
with *Friskies*

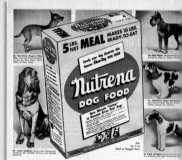

5 LBS. NET **MEAL** MAKES 10 LBS. READY-TO-EAT

Nutrena
DOG FOOD

Now! Nutrena's Exclusive New Miracle LIVIN
Gives Your Dog the Benefits of Amazing N
ANTIBIOTICS

Get Nutrena Dog Food at your STAF-O-LIFE or Nutrena Feed De

518
The Morris Animal Foundation and Hill's Diets

The first Seeing Eye dog, Buddy (see page 206), owned by Morris Frank, suffered from kidney disease. His veterinarian, Dr. Mark Morris of Edison, New Jersey, discovered that Buddy's condition could be managed by a special low-salt, low-protein diet of dry cereals, vitamins, and minerals along with fresh cottage cheese, fat, and meat. Since he was blind, Morris Frank found it difficult to make this special preparation, so Dr. Morris's wife would mix Buddy's special diet. Soon the Morris family could no longer meet the growing demand for the special kidney diet from other veterinarians, so an arrangement was made with the Hill Packing Company to package it.

This new concept of dietary management of canine disease was expanded to liver and heart disease, obesity, and pancreatitis. This was the beginning of Hill's Prescription Diets and the use of clinical nutrition for dogs. The contract with Dr. Morris stipulated that one-half cent per can would go to the Buddy Foundation, named for Morris Frank's guide dog. Dr. Morris commented, "For years animals have been used for medical research into human ills, and now it's time that something was done for the animals themselves."

The Buddy Foundation was renamed the Morris Animal Foundation, and today it is a major source of funds for humane animal health studies worldwide. Through its grants, it has been responsible for many significant breakthroughs for the health and well-being of companion animals and wildlife.

SPRATT'S DOG CAKES

The Standard Dog Food

AVOID Sweetened, Soft, or Medicated Foods; they cause indigestion, loss of coat, and many other evils.

Send stamp for "Dog Culture," which contains much valuable information.

SPRATT'S PATENT, Ltd.
Factories and Chief Offices at Newark, N. J.

Depots at San Francisco, Cal.; St. Louis, Mo.; Cleveland, Ohio; Montreal, Canada, Boston. Superintendents Factories also in London, England.

For more than 50 years
SPRATT'S
have held the
PREMIER POSITION
of **DOG FOODS** throughout
est is the cheapest.
mp for "Dog Culture"
Limited, Newark, N. J.

A square meal for your DOG and a square deal for your POCKETBOOK
SPRATT'S
DOG CAKES and
PUPPY BISCUITS
are made as only SPRATT'S know
Write for samples and send 2c. s
SPRATT'S PATENT, LTD

Spratt's Dog Cakes ARE THE BEST AND CHEAPEST
Send for FREE Catalog, "Dog Culture," which contains practical chapters on the feeding, kenneling, and general management of dogs, also chapters on cats.
SPRATT'S PATENT (Am'n) LTD. Newark, N. J., St. Louis, Mo.; San Francisco, Cal. Cleveland, Ohio, Boston, Mass., Montreal, Can.

519
Spratt's Dog Cakes

James Spratt, an electrician from Ohio, sailed to England in 1860 to sell lightning rods. As he disembarked, he noticed the dogs on the dock eating leftover hardtack sea biscuits. He knew he could provide a better product. SPRATT'S Biscuits gained immediate popularity since they were made with wheat flour, vegetables, beetroot, and meat.

One of James Spratt's salesmen was none other than Charles Cruft, the founder of the Crufts Dog Show, the largest dog show in the world. Cruft used to visit the kennels of large country estates and provide them with the very best prepared food for their dogs. He encouraged the breeding of purebred dogs since those were the people most likely to use Spratt's Dog Cakes.

SPRATTS MEAT FIBRINE DOG CAKES:
"The backbone of the canine race. For over 60 years the standard dog food suitable for the largest dog down to the Airedale. They require a degree of mastication which ensures clear strong teeth, hard gums and a healthy system."

520 Pigs' ears

521 Charlee Bears

522 String cheese

523 Air-Dried Grass-Fed
Buffalo Liver Strips

524 Bowser's Best Buffalo Bites

525 Turkey Jerky

526 Salmon "Yummy Chummies"

527 Power Bones

528 Rawhide

529 Hot dogs

530 Milk-Bones

531 Appawstisers

532 Beggin' Strips
Bacon! Wag wag wag . . . it's BACON!
(Apparently, dogs don't know it's not bacon.)

533 Breathbuster

534 Yip Yap Dog Breath Mints

535 Frosty Paws:
The ice cream treat for dogs

536 Anything left on the coffee table

537 Homemade Dog Biscuits

2 CUPS WHOLE WHEAT FLOUR

½ CUP CORN MEAL

1 TEASPOON SALT

2 TEASPOONS BONE MEAL

2 TABLESPOONS
   VEGETABLE OIL

½ CUP SMOOTH
   PEANUT BUTTER

2 LARGE EGGS MIXED WITH
   ¼ CUP BEEF BROTH

Preheat oven to 350 degrees.

Combine the dry ingredients in a large bowl. Stir in oil, peanut butter, and egg mixture. Knead the dough for 2 to 3 minutes until it holds together well, adding more broth if the dough is too stiff. Let the dough rest for appoximately 30 minutes while you take your dog for a walk.

Roll dough out on a lightly floured surface. Cut into shapes with your favorite cookie cutter. Hearts, biscuits, stars, cats, and mailmen are popular with most dogs.

Arrange the biscuits on greased cookie sheets and bake for about 30 minutes until golden brown. Turn off the oven and allow the biscuits to dry in the oven overnight. When cool, they can be taste-tested on your favorite dog.

538
Enormous dog biscuits that make a dog's eyes light up

539
Being REALLY good
for a biscuit

540
The delight of being
served by humans

Silent film star Strongheart and Lady Jule

541
Tasty all-natural treats from Barbara's Canine Café in Charlotte, North Carolina

Peanut Butter Breath Mints the perfect after-dinner treat, these delicate heart-shaped cookies are made with crushed whole peanuts and minced mint.

Salmon and Cheese Bon-bons Alaskan salmon and shredded Parmesan cheese baked into a delicious snack.

Mini Pizza Treats topped with pureed tomatoes, herbs, and low-fat shredded Parmesan cheese.

542
The Three Dog Bakery

Dog lovers Dan Dye and Mark Beckloff set out to create the world's best dog biscuits, and they just may have done it. In the 1980s, commercially available dog biscuits were full of additives, chemicals, and preservatives. Dan and Mark wanted to make a healthier alternative that was better tasting, using all-natural ingredients. After months of research and experimenting with recipes, they finally called in the taste-testers: Dottie, Gracie, and Sarah. In 1989, they opened their first Three Dog Bakery, named for their three wonderful girls. An article in the *Wall Street Journal* was followed by calls from Oprah, *People* magazine, the *New York Times,* and hundreds of other publications. Today they have stores all over the country and several in Japan, a thriving mail-order business, two popular cookbooks, and The Gracie Foundation for neglected and abused dogs.

Sarah, Gracie, and Dottie

543 Yappertizers from the Three Dog Bakery Cookbook

544 Bark and Fetch cookies delivered each month

545 A personalized 1-pound, foot-long peanut butter Dino Bone

546 Testing a new recipe from the Tummy Rub Club

547 Beagle Bagels

548 Grrrrrrrranola

193

Working Like
a Dog

Dogs with Jobs

Dogs work side by side with emergency workers, customs officials, doctors, and people with disabilities, displaying their talent, courage, intelligence, and loyalty.

549 Search-and-rescue dogs

These dogs can search long after an area is contaminated by other searchers and civilians, because of their ability to discriminate a tremendous variety of scents. Add to that their athleticism, endurance, sensitive hearing, and night vision, and dogs are far more efficient than human searchers.

550 Sirius

This canine hero was the only dog to lose his life at the World Trade Center during the September 11, 2001, search-and-rescue efforts.

551 Bear

Bear was a brave Golden Retriever who aided in the relief efforts at the World Trade Center. His life is celebrated in the book *Bear, Heart of a Hero* by Scott Shields with Nancy M. West.

552
Disaster dogs

These dogs are trained to find victims buried from building collapse, earthquakes, hurricanes, and terrorist attacks. To be certified by the Federal Emergency Management Agency as a disaster dog, the dog must master a number of skills, such as staying in one spot for a long period of time without being distracted, finding a human in a barrel and barking for 30 seconds straight, searching and finding two people buried in rubble, and learning to perform a "focused bark alert" until the handler arrives.

Cowboy, a search-and-rescue dog, worked with FEMA at Ground Zero.

Roselle, with owner Michael Hingson, left, Salty, with owner Omar Rivera, center, and K9 Search and Rescue dog Appollo, with handler NYPD Officer Peter Davis, display their PDSA Dickin Medals.

553 Appollo

A member of the New York Police Department K9 Search and Rescue team, Appollo was on the scene with his partner, Police Officer Peter Davis, just fifteen minutes after the second World Trade Center tower collapsed.

554 Roselle and Salty

Roselle and Salty were two guide dogs who saved their owners just before the collapse of the World Trade Center. Roselle led her blind owner, Michael Hingson, down from the 78th Floor and out of the building to safety. Guide dog Salty refused to leave the side of her owner, Omar Rivera, and led him through broken glass, other debris, and ankle-deep water down 71 floors. Both dogs were trained by the Guiding Eyes for the Blind.

555 The PDSA Dickin Medal

The PDSA, Britain's leading veterinary charity, awards the Dickin Medal to animals displaying courage and devotion to duty while serving in the army or civil defense. It was awarded to three American dogs in March 2002. Appollo was chosen to receive the PDSA Dickin Medal on behalf of the more than 300 search-and-rescue dog teams that participated in recovery efforts at Ground Zero and the Pentagon. Roselle and Salty were honored for their bravery and courage.

556
**All the search-and-rescue
dogs at Ground Zero**
Over 300 teams of dogs and handlers came
from all over the country and worked tirelessly
in the rescue and recovery efforts that followed
the tragedy of September 11, 2001.

557 Avalanche dogs

They work with ski patrols to locate missing hikers, skiers, or hunters buried in the snow. The first use of American-trained search dogs to locate avalanche victims was in Washington State in 1969.

558 The heroic dogs of the Saint Bernard Monastery

For over 200 years, dogs worked with the monks of the Saint Bernard Monastery, rescuing over 2,000 people. Marroniers, or mountain guides, were assigned to travelers and were accompanied by dogs. Their broad chests were efficient in clearing paths through the snow, and they displayed an excellent sense of direction. They could find their way through fog and snowstorms, and had a sensitive enough nose to discover people buried in the snow.

559 Barry

The most famous dog to come from the Saint Bernard Monastery, he is credited with saving 40 people in the deep snows and avalanches of a high mountain pass. Barry lived in the monastery from 1800 to 1812. Legend has it that he was killed by the 41st person he tried to save, and it is even engraved on a massive tombstone at the entrance to the Cimetière des Chiens in Paris. However, he was actually taken to Bern, Switzerland, where he retired and lived out his last two years. In 1815, his body was preserved and put on exhibition at the Natural History Museum in Bern, where he remains today.

560 Trailing dogs

Trained to follow the path of a lost person such as Alzheimer's patients, these dogs pick up a scent from a sock or glove, and can work trails that are several days old.

561 Cadaver dogs

They locate dead bodies and alert their handlers to the presence of human remains.

A search-and-rescue dog working in the aftermath of Hurricane Katrina.

562 Water search dogs

They work from boats or along the beach to locate drowning victims. The development of the first specific training methods for the use of such air-scenting search dogs was in 1979.

563 Canine disaster-relief dogs

After Hurricane Charley hit Florida in 2004, the Salvation Army requested canine assistance. The effort was so successful that FEMA officially sanctioned canine disaster relief as psychological first aid for relieving anxiety among people suffering emotional stress.

564 The ACE Awards

Awards for Canine Excellence (ACE Awards) are presented each year by the American Kennel Club in the following five categories: Law Enforcement, Search and Rescue, Therapy, Service, and Exemplary Companion Dog. The stories of these dogs are shared at the AKC/Eukanuba National Championship Show, with each of the honorees and their dogs being rewarded for their heroism.

565 Trouble

Looking for Trouble? The co-winner of the 2004 "Paws to Recognize" award is a U.S. Customs Beagle named Trouble. Trouble was obtained from an animal shelter, and with his handler had seized 1,834 prohibited items by 2004. He has located both Mediterranean fruit flies and Caribbean fruit flies, preventing a potential disaster for Florida's citrus industry.

566 The Beagle Brigade

With their green jackets and wagging tails, they are famous for their acute sense of smell, curiosity, and high response to food. They remain unfazed by the commotion of an airport setting.

567
The dogs who work with
U.S. Customs

568 Xena

Currency-detection dogs are trained to find money being smuggled out of the country. One day after receiving her certification, Xena, in a routine traffic stop, alerted her handler, Sergeant Perry, to a duffle bag in the trunk of the 2005 Chevy Impala. It contained $45,030.

569 Explosive-detection dogs

Explosive-detection dogs are trained to check cargo, trucks, aircraft, luggage, and passengers for explosives.

570 Agriculture-detection dogs

These canines can detect fruits, vegetables, meats, and other prohibited items that may carry pests or animal or plant diseases that could impact U.S. agricultural resources.

571 BORSTAR canines

Border Patrol Search, Trauma, and Rescue teams are highly specialized units capable of responding to emergency search-and-rescue situations in the United States. These dogs are trained to locate a victim, return to the handler, and lead the handler back to the victim. This is called a recall-refind indication.

572 Jacko

Jacko was trained to detect concealed humans and narcotics. By 2005, this clever Belgian Malinois had alerted officials to 218 concealed humans; discovered over 33,700 pounds of marijuana, 816 pounds of cocaine, 10 pounds of heroin, and 36,089 doses and 523 pounds of other controlled substances; and is responsible for the seizure of $444,000 in drug-contaminated currency. He is the winner of the 2005 "Paws to Recognize" award.

573 Narcotics-detection dogs

They work at border entry points to find concealed narcotics. A narcotics dog can search a vehicle in about 20 seconds, where it would take a customs officer hours to do the same thing.

574 Arson-detection dogs

With their sensitive noses, they can pinpoint one-thousandth of a drop of accelerant used to start a fire.

575 Termite-detection dogs

576 Mold-detection dogs

With their ability to locate the source of mold spores in walls, mold dogs have become a popular alternative to traditional mold inspection. Researchers have found that the dogs can detect a scent that is present in the air in only 1 part per 2 billion, making them perfect for the job.

577 Earth dogs

Dogs such as Terriers provide an ecological way to eliminate groundhogs, moles, and woodchucks from your yard.

578 The Border Collie goose patrol

They provide environmentally safe, humane goose control for golf courses and public parks.

579 Guard dogs

580 Livestock guardians and sheepherding dogs

581 Faith

Winner of the Service Dog division of the ACE Awards in 2005 is Faith, a Rottweiler owned by Leana Beasley and trained by the Assistance Dog Club of Puget Sound. Faith was trained for seizure and cardiac alert and for mobility assistance, and she knows over 150 commands. Leana was heating up the teakettle on the stove, and when she went to reach for it, she fell to the floor, suffering a grand-mal seizure triggered by her medication. The dog, sensing the emergency, retrieved the phone and placed the receiver next to her owner. Faith saw that Leana was not responding, so she went to the base unit and hit the 911 emergency button, went back to the receiver, and started barking into the phone. Faith then recognized the flashing lights of the ambulance and unlocked the door to let the emergency workers in. This saved Leana's life. The most amazing part of the story is that the dog performed all these tasks without direction from her owner. The depth of caring your dog has can never be overestimated.

582
The Seeing Eye

In 1927, Dorothy Harrison Eustis visited a school in Germany where dogs were being trained as guides for blind World War I veterans. She was so impressed that she wrote about this school in the November 5, 1927, *Saturday Evening Post,* in an article titled "The Seeing Eye."

Morris Frank, blind since the age of 16, had the article read to him, and he wrote to Mrs. Eustis asking her to train a dog for him so he could have the independence only a guide dog could bring to his life. Frank went to Switzerland in 1928 to attend L'Oeil Qui Voit, Mrs. Eustis's training school in Vevey. He returned with a trained dog named Buddy. They were the subject of much publicity, especially after he crossed the busiest street in New York City to show the world the trust he had in Buddy.

In 1929, Dorothy Eustis returned to the United States and, with Morris Frank, started The Seeing Eye for dogs and owners in Nashville. The first graduating class had two students. By December she had trained 17 teams. Now located in Morristown, New Jersey, the school continues to train dogs and their blind companions to work together and care for each other.

In addition to training dogs, the school maintains one of the foremost breeding programs in the country, providing valuable information on canine reproduction and genetics. Dogs are bred for health, temperament, and specific training abilities. Records are maintained on every puppy who is born into the program. Seeing Eye puppies go to live with volunteer families who raise the puppy for the first 18 months. At that age, the dog is brought back to the school for an intensive four-month training program, followed by an additional three to four weeks of training with their blind person. Dogs are taught to guide their blind owner safely to their destination. They are also taught to use their judgment as to whether to obey a command.

Buddy and Morris went on to be a major influence in the creation of Hill's Dog Food and the Morris Animal Foundation. They were also the inspiration for a 1984 Disney film, *Love Leads the Way.*

Dorothy Harrison Eustis, founder of The Seeing Eye, poses with Parole and Nancy, two dogs trained at the school to lead blind people, in New Jersey on September 7, 1933.

583
The comfort offered by therapy dogs

Studies have shown that visits from therapy dogs can lower anxiety and improve heart and lung pressure among heart-failure patients.

Bart, a five-year-old Australian Shepherd, pa[y]s a visit to a cardiac patien[t]

584 Canine Companions for Independence

This organization trains assistance and service dogs. Graduates of this program can pull wheelchairs, retrieve dropped items, and assist with grocery shopping. These specially trained dogs can open and close doors, turn lights on and off, use the phone to call for medical assistance, and thus provide independence for people with disabilities. CCI also trains facility dogs for schools, rehabilitation programs, and psychiatric centers. These dogs are used to help arthritis patients, by petting and grooming the dogs. Throwing a ball can help to rehabilitate an injured shoulder. The dogs also provide an important connection for autistic children, who will often play with a dog long before interacting with other people.

585 Cancer detection dogs

Dogs have recently been enlisted in the war against cancer. With their incredible sense of smell, and with proper training, the dogs in a recent study were able to correctly detect 99% of the lung cancer samples they were shown. They are also having success with breast and bladder cancer and melanomas.

586 Hearing dogs

Hearing dogs are trained to alert their owners to the telephone, doorbell, smoke and fire alarms, a crying baby, and other sounds requiring a response. Roy Kabat, an animal trainer for the movies and TV, founded Dogs for the Deaf in 1977, using dogs rescued from animal shelters.

587 Seizure-alert dogs

They are born with the ability to sense the onset of a seizure in a person, anywhere from seconds to hours before an episode. When a dog recognizes the symptoms, he will bark, paw at the owner so the person can get to a safe place, circle the person, prevent him from falling, or use a quick-dial pad on the phone to alert medical personnel.

588 Paws for Reading

It was found that autistic children and people who stutter are much more at ease when they read to a dog. Their disabilities are lessened when they communicate with a loving canine.

The Dogs of War

Military dogs are a unique combination of courage, devotion, intelligence, and loyalty. And they have surely helped to change the course of history. They march with generals and protect wounded soldiers. They serve many roles in the military, and have done so for thousands of years.

589 Sentry dogs

They accompany the military on patrol and in the foxholes and warn soldiers of the approaching enemy. Their mission: "Detect, detain, and destroy."

590 Messenger dogs

Messenger dogs saved thousands of lives during wartime by transporting information when other forms of communication were impossible or unsafe. They learned to jump foxholes, trenches, and barbed wire to deliver their messages.

591 The dogs of mercy

Casualty dogs detect wounded and dead soldiers in the field.

592 Ratters

Terriers were used as ratters in order to keep the trenches clear of rodents.

593 Mascots

With the ability to boost morale, the mascot brought humanity to the soldier.

"When you think of liberty
and count the reasons you are free . . .
Don't forget to think of me!"

from "When You Think of Liberty, Think of Me,"
a poem by Kathy Anne Harris honoring war dogs

"He is your friend,
    your partner, your
    defender, your dog.

You are his life, his
    love, his leader.

He will be yours,
    faithful and true,
    to the last beat
    of his heart.

You owe it to him to
    be worthy of such
    devotion."

— Anonymous

General George Custer was a true lover of dogs. One soldier commented, "I think he talked to the dogs all the time," and described him as looking "like a human island in a rolling sea of hounds." Especially fond of the coursing breeds, Custer had 40 dogs in all by the end of his career in 1876. His favorite dog, Tuck, died by his side at the Battle of the Little Big Horn.

594 Sallie, a brindle Staffordshire Bull Terrier

The mascot for the 11th Pennsylvania Infantry Regiment during the Civil War, she stayed with her regiment through bad weather and tough battles, providing comfort and loyalty to the men. She would bark as loudly as she could at the Rebels.

595 Jack, a brown-and-white Bull Terrier

Jack, the 102nd Pennsylvania Regiment mascot, was captured—and his regiment exchanged a Confederate prisoner for his release.

596 Lieutenant Pfeiff's loyal dog

Lieutenant Pfeiff, a Union soldier, was killed in the battle of Shiloh. His widow went to Tennessee to locate her husband body and claim it for burial. She was unable to find anyone who could help he search the more than 10,000 dead, until large dog ran across the field to her side. He was her husband's dog. He led her to an unmarked grave, which turned out to be that of her husband.

597 Cigarette dogs

In World War I, cigarette dogs were used to deliver cartons of cigarettes to the troops.

598 Rags, hero of World War I

On Bastille Day, 1918, a young Terrier was found in a pile of rags in the streets of Montmartre. Appropriately named Rags, he went on to an illustrious military career. During one of the campaigns against the Germans, Rags was used to send lifesaving messages between the 1st Infantry Division and the 7th Field Artillery. He also served as an early-warning system. With his superior hearing, he could anticipate the mortar attacks before the soldiers did. After the war, Rags was taken to America, where he died at the age of 20.

599 Stubby, the most decorated war dog in U.S. history

This courageous Bull Terrier mix served overseas for a year and a half during World War I. One night, Stubby caught a German spy in the camp and attached himself to the spy's bottom. He also saved his troops from a gas attack. For his war efforts, he was awarded Life Membership in the American Legion and the Red Cross.

600
Smoky: "Yorkie Doodle Dandy"

Smoky, a 4-pound Yorkshire Terrier, was the heroic dog of New Guinea, Borneo, and the Philippines. Adopted by Bill Wynne while stationed in New Guinea, Smoky spent 18 months in combat during World War II and flew on 12 combat missions with the third Emergency Rescue Squad. She entertained the troops in camps and hospitals. Her amazing story is told in Wynne's book, *Yorkie Doodle Dandy*. In November 2005, a permanent memorial was dedicated to "Smoky, Yorkie Doodle Dandy, and Dogs of All Wars" in the Cleveland Metroparks, Lakewood, Ohio.

601 Chips, a hero of World War II

Chips was a mixed breed and among the first dogs sent overseas for the war. He served in eight campaigns and survived them all. Starting with General George Patton in the African campaigns, he went on to Sicily with the 7th Army. After the troops established a beachhead, the dog, sensing the enemy nearby, disappeared across the field and was later found in an enemy foxhole holding on to the gunner by the throat. The other five men had their hands up in surrender to this fierce canine soldier.

Chips was also the sentry dog for Prime Minister Winston Churchill and President Franklin D. Roosevelt at the 1943 Casablanca Conference. Chips received the Silver Star and the Purple Heart for his war efforts. Shortly afterward, the awards were rescinded with a statement that awarding these medals to a canine demeaned them. Chip's troops gave him a jacket and placed their own medals on the dog to show their appreciation for his heroism.

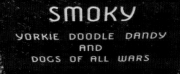

...l Wynne at the Smoky ...emorial dedication, ...ovember 2005.

SMOKY

YORKIE DOODLE DANDY
AND
DOGS OF ALL WARS

The Devil Dogs trained to accompany the Marines in landing operations, sentry duty, messages and first aid. Andy (below), one of the Devil Dog heroes, saved a tank platoon from annihilation by uncovering two machine gun nests in the dense jungle.

602 The Devil Dogs of the Marines

Trained at Camp Lejeune, the Devil Dogs fought with the Marines in the liberation of Guam. In all, 25 dogs gave their lives and are buried in the War Dog Cemetery there. The sculpture *Always Faithful* by Susan Bahary Wilner is dedicated to the memory of these courageous dogs:

Kurt	Yonnie	Koko	Bunkie
Skipper	Poncho	Tubby	Hobo
Ni	Prince	Fritz	Emmy
Missy	Cappy	Duke	Max
Blitz	Arno	Silver	Brockie
Bursch	Pepper	Ludwig	Rickey
Tam (buried at sea off Asan Point)			

603
Dogs are the eyes and
ears of the soldier

U.S. Marine Corps Raiders and their dogs, who were used for scouting and running messages,
start off for the jungle front lines on Bougainville in November 1943.

604 Sinbad of the Coast Guard

In 1938, the crew of the Coast Guard cutter *Campbell* adopted a mixed-breed puppy they named Sinbad. This salty sea dog became famous throughout the world for his bravery at sea during World War II, as well as his behavior in port.

His biography, written by fellow Coast Guardsman George R. Foley, made him an international celebrity and *Life* magazine reported on his fondness for bars and his "girls in every port."

Although Sinbad caused international incidents in Greenland and Casablanca, he was considered a brave sailor and earned the respect of his fellow crewmen during a battle with a Nazi submarine. He would serve aboard the *Campbell* for eleven years before retiring to the Barnegat Light Station in New Jersey. It was there that he passed away on December 30, 1951, and was laid to rest beneath the flagpole.

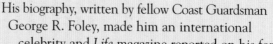

A salty seafarer savoring his suds. Sinbad, known in over 100 world ports for his ability to consume beer, enjoys a brew at Kubel's Bar, Barnegat Light.

One writer summed it up best when he wrote, "Perhaps that's why Coast Guardsmen love Sinbad. He's as bad as the worst and as good as the best of us."

218

605 Maximillian Talisman

This Boxer was another mascot for the Coast Guard, serving seven years at sea on a cutter and achieving the rank of chief boatswain's mate. Upon his retirement, he was "piped off" his cutter for the final time with full naval honors. During his career, he crossed the International Date Line twice and earned the United Nations medal, the Korean Service Medal, and the National Defense Service Medal.

606 Oliver

Born on the Coast Guard icebreaker *Northwind*, Oliver followed in his mother's pawsteps to become the ship's mascot.

607 Skunk

Skunk served as mascot of the Coast Guard icebreaker *Eastwind* in the 1940s.

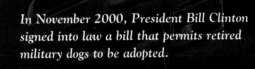

608
The well-trained dogs of the
Army, Navy, Air Force, and
Marine Corps

*In November 2000, President Bill Clinton
signed into law a bill that permits retired
military dogs to be adopted.*

K9 Promise:

"My eyes are your eyes, to watch and protect you and yours.

My ears are your ears, to hear and detect evil minds in the dark.

My nose is your nose, to scent the invader of your domain.

And so you may live,

My life is also yours."

—Anonymous

Showing Off

"You can do anything if
you have enthusiasm."
—Henry Ford

612
Sizing up the
competition

611
Watching the judges
deliberate over
the entry

Best in Show

From the first match show to international competition, it only takes one dog to beat you.

COLISEUM
MARCH 12 TO 15
ADMISSION 50¢
CHICAGO KENNEL CLUB'S
DOG SHOW

623
Having the
dog show
photographer
shoot the perfe
photo of your do

228

636
Learning what white-yellow-red-blue means

637
And getting lots of blue ribbons!

638
Crufts, the largest dog show in the world

Charles Cruft, an ambitious young man, began his career as a traveling salesman selling Spratt's "dog cakes." In 1878, just two years out of college, he was invited to organize the promotion of the canine section of the Paris Exhibition. During this period of the late 1800s, dog shows were privately owned ventures and were rather profitable, which appealed greatly to Cruft.

The very first Crufts show was held in 1891 at the Royal Agricultural Hall, Islington, England. After his death, the show was sold to the Kennel Club and continues to be run under its jurisdiction to this day.

Today's Crufts show is held each year in March at the National Exhibition Centre in Birmingham, England. It is the largest-attended dog show anywhere, with over 120,000 visitors and 21,000 dogs from all over the world. The show has been expanded to four days and is a virtual smorgasbord of vendors, dogs, exhibitions, and ceremonies covering ten indoor acres.

639
Meeting new friends on
the bench at Crufts

640
Watching Mary Ray's Heelwork to Music

Mary Ray is a pioneer in the sport of Canine Freestyle, or Heelwork to Music. Her performances before Best in Show in the Main Ring at Crufts have been broadcast live around the world, and many come to the show just to see Mary's latest routines.

The routine done to the overture of *Mack and Mabel* featured four Border Collies working together under command. Other famous routines through the years include *Harry Potter*, *Lord of the Dance*, and Fred Astaire's *Top Hat*. In addition to these exhibitions, Mary competes in Obedience and Agility at Crufts with her Shelties and Border Collies and has won both events multiple times.

An American show favorite, Co-Co the Norfolk Terrier, Am. and Eng Ch. Cracknor Cause Celebre, handled by Peter Green, won the prestigious Best in Show Keddel Memorial Trophy at Crufts.

641
The pomp and circumstance of Best in Show

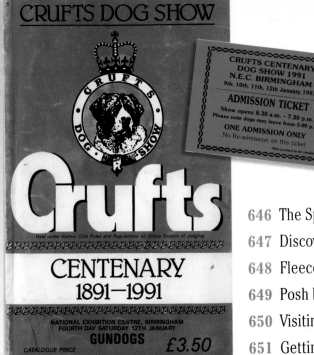

642 Meeting breeders from other countries

643 Visiting the overseas lounge for tea

644 The white gloves presenting the trophies

645 Streakers

646 The Special Event Rings

647 Discovering Discover Dogs

648 Fleece piled 10 feet high

649 Posh beds

650 Visiting all the halls at least once

651 Getting lost in the halls at least once

652 Viewing the exhibitions from the Pedigree booth

653 Sitting ringside on the floor

654 Finding your favorite breed in the benching area

655 Exhibitors wearing their ribbons

656 Seeing a Challenge Certificate

657 The Kennel Club Art Auction

658 Watching Golden Retrievers all day long

235

659
Westminster

The Westminster Breeding Association began as a club in 1876. A group of gentlemen who hunted with their sporting dogs named their club after a favorite hotel where they would have their meetings. Later that year they changed the name to the Westminster Kennel Club and decided to hold a dog show. It was titled "The First Annual New York Bench Show of Dogs."

The original show was held in 1877 at Gilmore's Garden on Madison Avenue in New York City. Dogs were listed in the catalog as either "not for sale" or for sale at prices ranging from $50 to $10,000. The entry fee was $2, and that included feed and care of the dogs entered. Seven years later, the Westminster Kennel Club became the very first member group of the American Kennel Club, and afterward all dogs being shown at Westminster were required to be registered with the American Kennel Club. Registration applications were accepted, with few restrictions, for a fee of 50 cents.

Famous names have often appeared in the roster of entries for Westminster, including Lou Gehrig, Bill Cosby, Martha Stewart, and Greg Louganis. Today, the winner of Best in Show at Westminster has to be prepared to party and make the rounds of the morning and talk TV shows. Everyone loves a winner.

660
Sensation

Sensation, the famous lemon and white Pointer, was purchased by George DeForest Grant, a charter member of the WKC, in 1876 and brought over from England. His pedigree says "property of Westminster Kennel."

He was an exceptional example of his breed in both field and conformation, known for his outstanding nose, magnificent head, and elegant style, and he was made the official mascot of the club.

The image in use today on the front of the Westminster Catalog was modeled on an engraving by W. Wellstood & Co.

237

661
Getting into Westminster

671
A weathered tack box

681 Dog show gear:

Grooming table, grooming apron sporting your favorite dog food logo, the tack box, scissors, brushes and combs, stripping blades, show leads and collars in just the right color, creams, mousse, powder, pomades

682
Being ready for
your close-up

699
Being able to make a
stunning dog look even
more beautiful

The 2004 Best in S
winner Newfoundla
Ch. Darbydale's All
Pouch Cove (Josh),
Michelle Ostermille

700
The excitement when the judge awards Best in Show

ABOVE: *John Oulton with 1999 Best in Show winner Ch. Loteki Supernatural Being (Kirby), a Papillon*

OBEDIENCE

701 Being able to heel—even outside the ring

702 Having your agility dog take only *one* of the jumps
in the Obedience Ring

703 The wag of the tail for a job well done

704 Successful sits and downs even when the dog next to yours
breaks the stay

705 Making costumes for team obedience

706 Finding the right article right away

707 Having your dog bail you out

708 Doing the perfect figure eight

709 Finding the perfect dumbbell

710 And picking it up

711 Showing off your manners

712 Teaching humility

713 Teamwork

714 Getting a 199½

715 Getting your handler to smile
through her nervousness

716 Getting High in Trial with your veteran dog

717 Being invited to the International Competition at Crufts

718 Getting your title in three straight shows

719
Practice makes
perfect

AGILITY

FIELD

Lure coursing was developed as a safer, more controlled alternative to hunting rabbits in open fields. The hounds chase plastic bags on a course laid out to simulate the random zigzag path of escaping game. The hounds are judged on enthusiasm, ability to follow the lure, speed, agility, and endurance.

The word Terrier comes from the Latin *terra*, which means "earth."

Terriers are bred to burrow and flush out vermin and fox from their underground dens.

The sport of skiing while being pulled by your dog, or a team of dogs. The person with the most dogs has the right-of-way.

The Overachievers

From a 4-ounce Yorkie to a 343-pound Mastiff, dogs are setting records and amazing us every day. Here are a few of the best and the brightest.

774 Smallest dog

Danka Kordak Slovakia is much smaller than her name. Residing in Slovakia, she is the world's smallest living dog in terms of length, measuring only 7.4 inches long.

Whitney, a Yorkshire Terrier, is the shortest dog, measuring a mere 3 inches tall. The previous record holder was also a Yorkie who was only 2.5 inches at the shoulder and weighed only 4 ounces, about the size of a box of matches.

775 Tallest dog

A therapy dog named Millenium's Rockydane Gibson, a harlequin Great Dane, measures 42.2 inches tall when standing on all four legs, making him the tallest dog.

When he stands on his hind legs, he stretches up to over 7 feet tall.

776 Heaviest dog ever

When Zorba lived in the United Kingdom in 1989, he weighed in at 343 pounds. This Mastiff was 8 feet 3 inches from nose to tail!

777 Biggest dog wash

It took just 8 hours and 12 people to wash 848 dogs, setting the record for Australia's biggest dog wash, in Sydney, on September 14, 2003.

778 Largest litter

Tia, a Neapolitan Mastiff, gave birth by Cesarean section to 24 puppies on November 29, 2004. She is owned by Damian Ward and Anne Kellegher of Manea, England.

779 Best tracker ever

Sauer, a Doberman Pinscher trained by Detective-Sergeant Herbert Kruger, tracked a thief across the Great Karoo in South Africa, a distance of 100 miles.

780 What big ears you have!

Mr. Jeffries, a Basset Hound in West Sussex, England, measures in at 11.5 inches per ear. As the longest in the world, his ears are insured for $48,000. His registered name is Knightsfollie Ladiesman, and he is the grandson of Biggles—who was the face of Hush Puppies shoes!

781 Largest dog show

The largest dog show is Crufts, held each year at the National Exhibition Centre in Birmingham, England.

782 Highest jump by a dog

At the Purina Dog Chow Incredible Dog Challenge in Gray Summit, Missouri, Cinderella May A Holly Grey, trained by Lourdes Edlin and Sally Roth of Purina and owned by Kathleen Conroy and Kate Long of Miami, Florida, set the dog Puissance record by clearing a 66-inch jump. Cindy made her flight on October 3, 2003.

783 Most jump rope skips by a dog

Olive Oyl, a Russian Wolfhound from Grays Lake, Illinois, holds the dog jump rope record of 63 jumps in one minute.

784 Highest dog tire climb

Arnold Funk's dog, Duke, a Border Collie and Australian Shepherd cross, jumped into a 9-foot-deep stack of tires to retrieve a small toy.

785 Highest sky-diving dog

Brutus, a miniature red smooth Dachshund, is a certified skydiver. With his owner, Ron Sirull, he has made over 100 jumps including a record fall of 15,000 feet.

786 Most tennis balls in a dog's mouth

Who else but a Golden Retriever? Augie, owned by the Miller family of Dallas, Texas, stuffed five regulation-sized tennis balls in her mouth and won a trip to New York for the *Late Show with David Letterman*.

787 Fastest car window opened by a dog

In 11.34 seconds, a Border Collie named Striker, owned and trained by Francis Gadassi of Hungary, set the record for opening a nonautomatic car window.

788 Oldest dog

Bluey, an Australian Cattle Dog, worked cattle and sheep for over 20 years in Australia. He lived a total of 29 years and 5 months.

789
The World's Smartest Dog®

Chanda-Leah, a Toy Poodle from Hamilton, Ontario, Canada, has a repertoire of over 1,000 hand and verbal commands. She is the Guinness record holder for "Most Tricks Performed by a Dog." Chanda can play the saxophone, paint in watercolors, untie your shoelaces, get you a Kleenex if you sneeze, and set the table. When she is finished playing, she will put away her toys. And if that's not enough, she knows the days of the week, the months of the year, the alphabet, and the numbers from 1 to 100, can add, subtract, and multiply, and can read all of the above from cue cards.

Chanda has received numerous awards, and has appeared on television and in magazines. With her owner, Sharon Robinson, she entertains in schools, churches, nursing homes, and hospitals, brightening the lives of the people she meets and sharing her energy and enthusiasm for life.

Here are a few of the nearly 1,100 tricks that Chanda-Leah can do . . .

Shake hands
Smile
Wave like Lassie
Sit pretty
Get on your spot
Turn around once on your spot
Turn around twice on your spot
Ring the bell
What do you do when you see a cat?
What do you do when you see a big dog?
What does a sad puppy look like?
Show me your sore paw
Do you have a kiss for Mommy?
Do you love me? . . . Show me
Do you have a container for the rose?
Lie down
Lie down . . . on your side
Bark . . . louder
Roll over
Again (Understands the word 'again' for a repeat of any trick)
Back up
Body shake
Sneeze
Set the table (she brings napkin and dish)
Fetch the spoon
Fetch the fork
Remove the bow from your teddy bear
Ah choo!—brings Kleenex
Fetch & carry—fetches ball
Put the ball in my hand
Put the ball in the can
Play the piano—la, la, la, on the grand piano
Untie knot
Untie three knots

Want to go for a walk?—fetches collar and
    leash
It's cold outside—fetches sweater
Would your puppy like to go for a walk?
Pull out your toy box
Pick up your toys and put them away
Jump through the hoop
Shell game—finds the peanut
Put the peanut in my hand
Look in the mirror
Go to your mat
Go to the door
Open the door
Close the door
Pick up the garbage
Fetch the letter addressed to "Mommy"
Fetch the letter addressed to "Chanda"
Did the mailman bring any other mail?—fetches
    mail with the word "junk" written on it
What do you do with "junk" mail?—drops it in
    the garbage bucket
My toes are cold, bring my socks
Bring my slippers
Get up on your barrel . . . sit
Get off your barrel
Cookies & tea—holds a teacup on head, and a
    cookie on nose
What do you take to a pajama party?—runs
    and fetches pajamas
What else do you take?—a blanket
Do you want to take your teddy bear?—
    fetches her teddy bear
Look out the window
Where's your Easter bonnet?
Jump rope

Chanda's piano
Roll the barrel—14.5"
Roll the barrel—10"
Roll the barrel—4.5"
Roll the barrel—2.5"
Roll the barrel—1"
Go to my purse and bring . . .
. . . Kleenex
. . . Wallet
. . . Candy
. . . Glasses
Return the . . . Kleenex, etc.
Close my purse
Take the bunny to your wagon
Put the bunny in the wagon
Bring me the wagon
Bring me a Crispy Crunch
Bring me a Kit Kat
Bring me a Wunderbar
Bring me a Caramilk
Get the green ball—sit on the green spot
Get the yellow ball—sit on the yellow spot
Get the pink ball—sit on the red spot
Roll the "little" ball with your nose
Roll the "big" ball with your nose
Get on the red mat
Get on the yellow mat
Get on the green mat
Bring me the green ball
Bring me the yellow ball
Bring me the pink ball
Put your paw "on" your nose—hold it
Limbo
Play the saxophone
Take a bow

790
The world's largest dog biscuit

Baked in 2004 by Jerald and Lisa
Richardson of Stanwood,
Washington, this massive cookie
was 8 feet long, 30 inches wide,
and 2 inches thick and weighed
300 pounds. The recipe included
garlic, parsley, whole-wheat flour,
wheat germ, carrots, margarine,
and water, topped with an egg wash
and Parmesan cheese.

Buck

Skywalker and friends

Walker and Maverick

Wrigley

Sam

Channel

Poochini

Chip and

Goldie

Joey

Hannibal

Lucy

Pugsey

Amber

Jerry

Chance, Tommie,
and Teaka

Gordon

Hope

Faith

Rocky

Scooter

John Boy

Piper

Haley and Kayla

Drake

Best Friends

"Dogs are not our whole life,
but they make our lives whole."
—Roger Caras

Sparkle

Scottie

Dixie

Oliver

Maggie

Diesel

Schooner

Belle and Teigh

Yukon

First Dogs

Even those in the White House make time for their beloved pets.
In fact, it helps to love dogs when you want to get elected.

791 Washington's Foxhounds

George Washington, the Father of Our
Country, is also considered the Father
of the American Foxhound. His original
hounds came from England in the
1770s. He later received a gift of French
Hounds from the Marquis de Lafayette.
Their voices in the field were said to
be like the bells of Moscow.

**792 Jefferson's Briards:
the first dogs to be licensed**

Thomas Jefferson was a breeder of
Briards, brought from France to guard his
sheep at Monticello. Jefferson started dog
licensing to help identify hounds that
were destroying livestock near his home.

793 Lara Buchanan

James Buchanan's Newfoundland, Lara,
was well known for the ability to sleep
with one eye open and the other one
shut. One newspaper wrote that Lara was
"remarkable for his immense tail and his
attachment to his master."

794 Fido Lincoln

Abraham Lincoln's mixed-breed dog,
Fido, was the first presidential dog
known to be photographed. Fido, left
with neighbors in Springfield, Illinois,
when the Lincolns moved into the
White House, is credited as the
inspiration for the famous Lincoln
quote "Calling a tail a leg doesn't
make it a leg."

795 Veto Garfield

James Garfield named his dog Veto as
a warning to Congress.

796 Dash Harrison

Benjamin Harrison's Collie, Dash, had
a doghouse of his own, right next to
the White House.

797 The Hayes dogs

Dot, a Cocker Spaniel; Jet, a small
black dog; Hector, the Newfoundland;
Grim, the Greyhound; Deke, the
English Mastiff; Juno and Shep, the
hunting dogs; and two Shepherds all
enjoyed quality time with President
Rutherford B. Hayes.

> **"Any man who does not like dogs and want them about, does not deserve to be in the White House."**
>
> —Calvin Coolidge

798 Pete Roosevelt

Teddy Roosevelt, a great animal lover, had many dogs running around the White House. Pete, a Bull Terrier, was probably the most mischievous of the group and often chased the cabinet officers. He was sent off to the family estate in New York after he ripped the pants off the French ambassador, Jules Jusserand.

799 Rob Roy Coolidge: "speaking" at press conferences

Rob Roy, President Calvin Coolidge's beloved white Collie, would accompany the president to the office in the afternoon and to his weekly press conferences. The Collie reportedly enjoyed vocalizing during these proceedings.

800
Laddie Boy Harding

Laddie Boy, an Airedale owned by Warren G. Harding, was a celebrity during his time in the White House. He had his own chair at cabinet meetings and was interviewed by the *Washington Post* in 1921. He enjoyed retrieving golf balls on the White House lawn, and he was the recipient of a magnificent birthday cake made of dog biscuits.

Laddie Boy survived the loss of his beloved master when Harding died only two years into his term. Then the thousands of members of the Newsboys Association each donated a penny; those pennies were melted down and cast into a statue of Laddie Boy, which now resides at the Smithsonian Institution in Washington, D.C.

801
Fala Roosevelt

Franklin D. Roosevelt's Scottish Terrier, Fala, was given a bone every morning, served on a silver tray with his master's breakfast. He accompanied the president to his favorite retreats, such as Hyde Park, in upstate New York, and Warm Springs, Georgia. But he was also present on the scene of many important political events, traveling on Air Force One and in Roosevelt's custom-made train car. Fala's image and personality were so associated with the Executive Office that he was featured in an MGM film about the White House and even became the subject of satirical cartoons entitled "Mr. Fala of the White House."

802 Begging for votes with King Tut

King Tut was Herbert Hoover's German Shepherd guard dog. In an effort to make him appear warm and

friendly, Hoover's campaign photos featured him smiling with his dog. King Tut used to patrol the White House at night to keep his master safe, and he became known as "the dog that worried himself to death."

803 Upstaging the first lady

Dwight D. Eisenhower's Weimaraner, Heidi, would jump up in front of the cameras and not allow the first lady to be photographed.

804 The dogs of Camelot

John F. Kennedy had many White House pets. Pushinka was a gift from the Russian premier, Nikita Khrushchev, and was the daughter of Strelka, one of the first of the Russian space dogs. Pushinka met up with Charlie, the Welsh Terrier, and produced a litter of puppies named "Pupniks" by the president.

805 Rex Reagan

Rex, the Cavalier King Charles Spaniel owned by President Ronald Reagan, had an elaborate white Colonial doghouse with red drapes, decorated with pictures of the president and first lady.

806 Writing your own best seller

Millie, the famous English Springer Spaniel of George H. W. Bush, had a best-selling book. The royalties were donated to the Barbara Bush Foundation for Family Literacy.

807
Getting to sing a duet
with the president

One of Lyndon Johnson's favorite dogs was Yuki,
a mixed-breed dog his daughter found at a gas
station in Texas. Yuki and the president entertained
many dignitaries by having a howling duet, much to
the delight of both dog and owner.

808 Richard Nixon's dogs

During his presidency, Nixon's best friends included King Timahoe, an Irish Setter; Pasha, a Yorkshire Terrier; and Vicky, a French Poodle. Nixon kept a stash of dog biscuits in his desk drawer in case anyone got hungry.

809 Liberty Ford

Liberty, Gerald Ford's Golden Retriever, was not well housebroken, and at 3 A.M. she needed to go out. The sleepy president donned his bathrobe and slippers and took Liberty to the south lawn of the White House. The Secret Service had secured the residence, and the locked-out president and his dog tried several staircase entrances before they were detected trying to break in.

810 Miss Beazley

This Scottish Terrier gets to romp with President George W. Bush and his older Scottie, Barney, on the White House lawn.

811
Not everyone obeys the president

Buddy, President Bill Clinton's Chocolate Labrador Retriever, arrived at the White House in 1997. His antics were much photographed, and he and the president shared some special moments.

Reflected Glory

From kings and queens to movie stars, famous people
find true acceptance and real love with their dogs.

812 Marie Antoinette's Papillons

The queen of France was very fond of her Papillons, and some say she gave them their name, which in French means "butterfly." The royal dogs' *niche à chien*—doghouse—at Versailles was made of wood and upholstered with turquoise silk. She went to the guillotine carrying her little dog, and afterward the dog was cared for in a building in Paris that today is called Papillon House.

813 Mary Queen of Scots' Skye Terrier

Mary loved animals, and she found comfort in her Skye Terrier while she was in prison. Her little dog was with her at her execution in 1587 and was found in the folds of her skirt, refusing to leave her.

814 The Pekingese of the emperors of China

The Pekingese was the constant companion of the Chinese emperors, leading processions, announcing his arrival, and carrying the emperor's train. In order to breed the most perfect dogs, the pregnant mothers were shown pictures of beautiful dogs, were surrounded by desired colors, and slept on thick sheepskin to encourage a thick coat. All-white dogs were especially prized and treated with respect. White being rare, and also the color of mourning, these dogs were believed to harbor the spirit of a great man.

815 Queen Victoria's Pomeranians

Throughout her life, Victoria had more than 15 different breeds of dogs. On a trip to Italy in 1888, she bought four Pomeranians, two of whom—Marco and Gina—went on to become champions at dog shows in London.

816 The Corgis of Queen Elizabeth II

As a young girl, Princess Elizabeth fell in love with a Welsh Corgi puppy owned by Viscount Weymouth. Within a few days, she had her own pup, named Dookie. Although the queen has shared her life with a number of breeds, the Welsh Corgi has been a royal favorite. It is reported that when the queen is at home, she fixes each dog's dinner, prepared to his or her individual taste.

817 Michaelangelo's Pomeranian

This fortunate dog watched art history unfold from his seat on a satin pillow, as his owner painted the Sistine Chapel.

818 Diamond

Sir Isaac Newton's Pomeranian, Diamond, is said to have knocked over a candle on his desk and destroyed a stack of papers containing 20 years of research.

819 Pepito

Bandleader Xavier Cugat often performed with Pepito, his tiny Chihuahua, in his pocket.

820 A dog named Beau

Actor Jimmy Stewart used to keep a lint brush by the front door to remove hair left on his guests' clothing by his Golden Retrievers. Stewart wrote a poem about his dog Beau, which began:

He never came to me when I would call
Unless I had a tennis ball,
Or he felt like it,
But mostly he didn't come at all.

Stewart truly loved his dog named Beau.

821 Ten famous Labrador lovers

Henry Kissinger, Kevin Costner, Harrison Ford, Frank Sinatra, E. B. White, Barbara Cartland, Sheryl Crow, Joan Rivers, Arnold Schwarzenegger, and Ronald Reagan

822 Four famous West Highland White Terrier lovers

Alfred Hitchcock, Pablo Picasso, Bo Derek, and Charles Darwin

823 Seven famous fans of Golden Retrievers

Mary Tyler Moore, Ron Perelman, Bernadette Peters, Jimmy Buffet, Indira Gandhi, Oprah Winfrey, and Bill Murray

824 Three famous Dachshund lovers

Brooke Astor, James Dean, and Andy Warhol

825 Betty White

Betty White is one of the most generous dog lovers and a trustee of the Morris Animal Foundation. With her late husband, Allen Ludden, she wrote and hosted one of the first animal shows on TV, *The Pet Set*. This talented actress carries her message of love of dogs, along with her famous smile, everywhere she goes.

826
Elvis and his dogs

Elvis Presley had a genuine love of animals and owned several dogs throughout his life. Baba, his Collie, appeared in films with Elvis. Edmund, a Pomeranian; Getlo, a Chow Chow; Muffin, a Great Pyrenees; Stuff and Teddy Bear, both Poodles; and Snoopy and Brutus, Great Danes, all shared their lives with the King. He is pictured here with Sweet Pea, a dog whom Elvis gave to his mother in 1956. After her death, Elvis continued to care for the dog.

827
The dogs of Sigmund Freud

Freud came to love dogs in the later part of his life. From Marie Bonaparte, a friend and breeder of Chow Chows, he received his first of many dogs. His dogs provided an outlet for open affection and playful fun, a welcome relief from the formality of the times. Freud hated birthdays, so his daughter would always arrange a party with the dogs—Jofi, Lun, and Tattoun—seated in chairs around the table, all wearing party hats. Attached to one of their collars would be an envelope with a poem inside written by the dog. Freud found fun in reading the poem and serving cake to the lucky dogs.

The dogs also helped him in his work. He often had Jofi in his office with him while he was seeing patients. By observing the dog's behavior, Freud could tell if a patient might be under stress (the dog would move over to the desk) or deeply depressed (the dog would move close to the couch, within reach of the patient). And 50 minutes after the session began, Jofi would rise and stretch and walk to the door!

Having been diagnosed with cancer shortly after World War I, Freud found great comfort in his canine companions during his last days.

828
It's Mine

Gaining possession of THE toy is most important. It doesn't matter how many toys are available. There is only ONE toy that matters. Once one dog wins, the loser often picks up a different toy—which becomes the new object of desire.

Dogs Just Want to Have Fun

The games dogs play can be very intricate, with rules that change in a heartbeat.

829 The Elbow Toss

This technique, mastered by many dogs, needs a sitting human and a dog. The dog eagerly awaits the human's hand being placed within reach and then maneuvers his nose under the hand. A quick flick of the nose propels the hand into the air, providing the opportunity for the dog to get his head onto the human's lap, perfectly positioned for petting.

830 Chasing the Water Drops

This involves leaping up in the air with abandon, trying to bite the stream of water when the hose is turned on.

831 Ambush

This is best played with two dogs, although it can be modified for dog and human. The dog hides behind a tree and waits for his playmate to pass close by. Then the dog comes out from his hiding place, nips the other dog in the butt, and runs away. There are many variations.

832 The Face Grab

Two dogs alternate in attempting to get as much of the other dog's face into his mouth as he can.

833 Shake When Wet

If you stand in front of a wet, shaking dog rather than to the side, you won't get as wet. All that extra skin rotates and takes on a life of its own, being able to propel water droplets up to 25 feet.

834 Pounce

Two dogs face off about 100 feet from each other. The length of the game depends on the initial distance apart. They each adopt a "Ta-Da" stance—alert, on guard, maybe even on point. The dogs imperceptibly move closer, never taking their eyes off each other. At about 10 feet apart, one dog breaks the mesmerizing standoff and, with one giant leap, pounces on his opponent.

835 T-Bone

Two dogs start perpendicular to each other, at least 20 feet apart. One dog is paying attention to the scents of the day. The other dog runs full tilt at him, hitting him in the ribs. Fun!

836 Nasty Face

Best friends lie next to each other on their side and try to look as mean and nasty as they can. This is accompanied by whining and the snapping of teeth but tempered with a wagging tail.

837 Catching Bugs

This is best with house-flies; sometimes, when bees are the object of this game, a nasty sting to the face can be the result.

838 Snowface

839
A full set of English
dog cigarette cards

All Things Dog

t all starts with one small item, and then it begins
to snowball. Dog lovers collect everything from
Christmas ornaments to oil paintings, as long as it
has an image of a dog.

853
Saying "I love you" with a
doggie valentine

865
Antique brass dog bookends to hold all your dog books

866

Hand-painted wood cutouts of dogs
made by your grandfather

867

Porcelain plant pots in the
shape of your special dog

868
Dog postcards

WHEN SHALL I GET
A LETTER FROM YOU?

877
Antique dog toys

878
Old packaging labels

879
A Mirasol Glassworks
stained-glass dog hung
in a sunny window

880
A handmade hooked rug,
perfect for nap time

881
A needlepoint
portrait of your
favorite dog
done by a
dear friend

882
A Pointer painted on
black velvet

883
A gallery of paint-by-
number dog portraits

Dog Years

Those of us fortunate enough to spend our lives
in the company of dogs can enjoy all the times in a dog's
life, from the wild happiness of puppyhood to the profound
connection we share with our older companion. One thing
is certain: the years go by too quickly.

884
Happiness is a
warm puppy

885
Wishing your toy do[g]
was a real puppy

886
Getting new doggy to[ys]
for your birthday

887
Being best friends with
the neighbor's dog

888
Believing your cousin's
dog looks just like
Rin Tin Tin

889
A stuffed dog to sleep
with every night

890
Hoping to be
adopted by a
wonderful
family

891 Meeting the breeder of
your new dog

892 Going to the animal shelter to
find just the right dog

893 Adopting a rescue dog

894 The kindness of taking in a
foster dog

895 Coming home with your new
best friend

896 Sleeping with your hand in
the crate to comfort the
new puppy

897 Choosing the bank that
gives dog treats at the
drive-through window

898 Finding the perfect collar
and matching leash

899 Lying on the floor and being
smothered with kisses

900 Sitting very still because the
puppy has fallen asleep in
your lap

901 Puppy love

902
The magical
moment when your
dog chooses you

> "Whoever said you can't buy
> happiness forgot about puppies."
> —*Gene Hill*

903 Thinking your name is "Oh, he's so cute!"

904 Growing into the size of your feet

905 Puppy breath

906 Being able to crowd the runt from a nipple

907 The drowsiness of a bellyful of warm milk

908 Digging out the water bowl

909 Getting caught in the act

910 A good ripping time with a sock

911 Discovering toilet paper

912 Peeing in the warm lap of a huma

925
Making new friends

926
Having your own spot

927
Testing your
limits

928
Going out and
coming back in.
Then going
out again.

935
The excitement of digging for nothing in particular

936
Tolerating
humiliation with
dignity and
grace

"Anybody who doesn't know what soap tastes like never washed a dog."

—Franklin P. Jones

937
Having the patience to accept the things that one cannot change

938
Going out on the town with your best friends

939
Following your nose

940
A leap that feels like flying

941 Greeting each day with boundless enthusiasm

942 Learning a new trick

943 Being in coat

944 Maturing

945 Knowing that you are loved

946 Competing at dog shows

947 Getting titles before and after your name

948 Experiencing the joy of being the perfect dog

949 Being trusted to have the run of the house

950 Enjoying all the hugs when you come back from the groomer

951 Knowing your special place in the home

952 Being part of the family

953 Bringing the leash so you can go for a walk

954 Riding like the masthead at the prow of the rowboat

955 Making peace with the cat

956 Never being late for dinner

957 Unexpected snacks under the table

958 Helping Mom with her diet by walking twice a day

959 A slobbery tennis ball dropped in your hand

960 Having the phone held to your ear so you can hear your person say, "I miss you!"

962
Getting to go on the family vacation

963
Finding your voice

961
Tummy rubs on demand

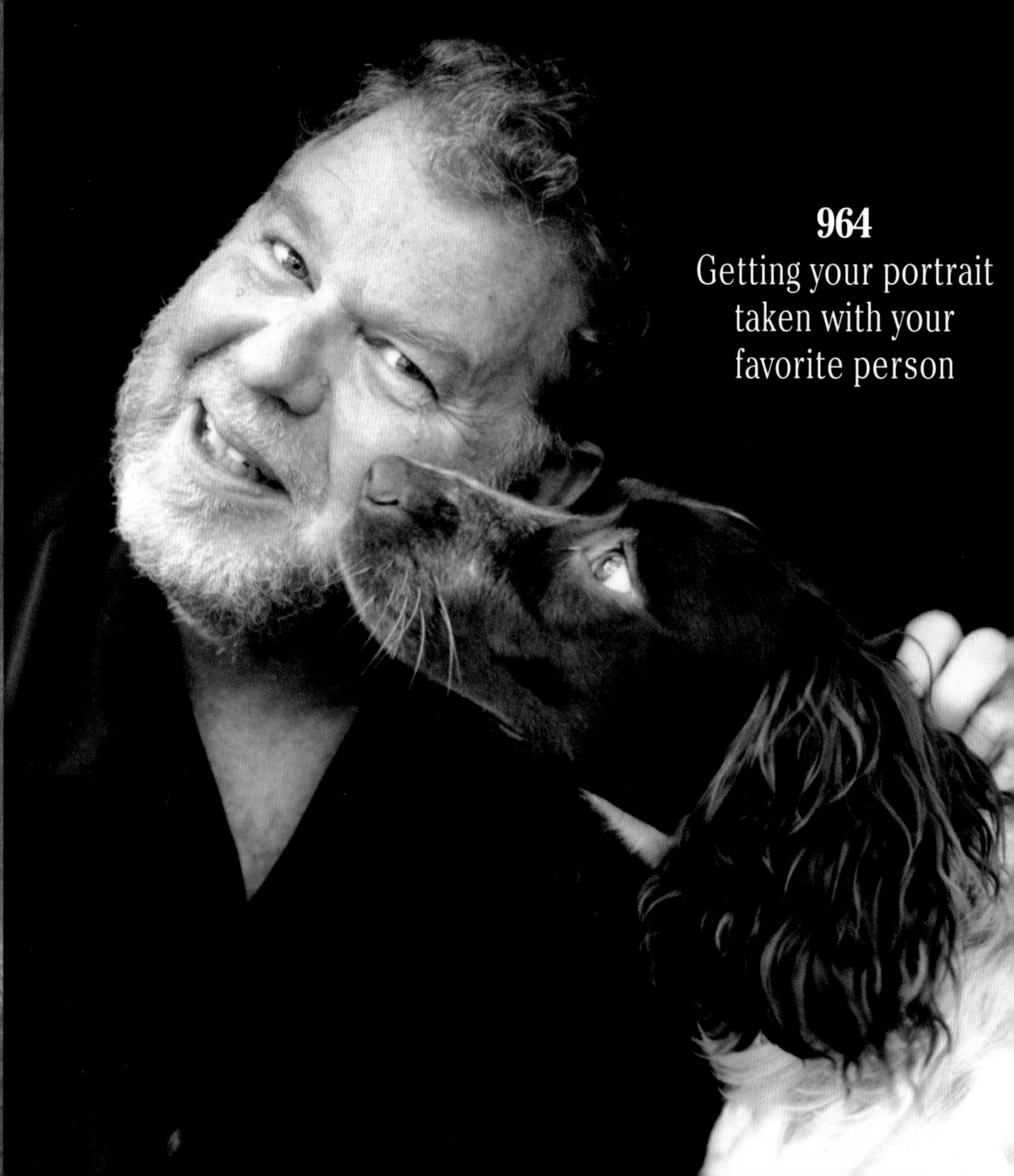

964
Getting your portrait
taken with your
favorite person

965
A lasting memory of your
special friendship

966
A surprising sense of calm after the wild years

967 Peaceful feelings

968 Understanding everything

969 Still wanting to play

970 Quiet moments together

971 Staying close by

972 Tilting your head to listen

973 Getting lost in their eyes

974 White around the muzzle

975 Sitting together by the fireplace

976 Knowing just how to comfort someone who is sad

977 Making you pay attention

978 A quiet, stubborn strength

979 Letting the squirrel cross the backyard

980 Choosing to heel rather than run out ahead

981 Senior diet!

"We never really own a dog as much as he owns us."
—*Gene Hill*

988
The nobility that comes with age

989

Dreaming of all the
squirrels that got away

990 Proving old dogs *can* learn new tricks

991 Thinking you look worldly with your new gray beard

992 Sleeping on the deck in a warm patch of sun

993 When a stretch and a yawn are as good as a walk

994 Stoically watching a young dog run circles around you

995 Trying to catch your tail just one more time

996 Telling a pup to just back off

997 Being comfortable with a few extra pounds

998 The old girl's bark

999 Knowing you're old but still top dog

1,000
Dogs teach us how to
love with an open heart,
and how to live in joy

1,001
Memories of our
special time together
will last a lifetime

Acknowledgments

The first thank you goes to Leslie Stoker, our publisher, and inspired Jennifer Levesque, our editor, for their love of dogs and belief in our project. And to Richard Slovak who wouldn't stop digging until he found all our typos! Thanks, as always, to Angela Escalante, for keeping us on track from beginning to end, and for her delicious homemade dog biscuits!

Next, we would like to thank George Berger, the publisher of the *AKC Gazette*, for his encouragement, for being busy, and for his generous help with our book.

A great big wag goes out to Sheri Seggerman, who went beyond her love of horses and shared with us her love of dogs. To Dr. Sue Ann Lesser, who helped with defining the breed characteristics on one of my pilgrimages to Pagey's house, and for knowing about the dogs in Gettysburg. To Rachel Page Elliott, who has forgotten more than most people will ever know.

To David Frei, who was generous beyond all expectations and shared the treasures of the Westminster Kennel Club with us. Thanks go to Samantha Gregory and everyone connected with Crufts for their kind help; to Abbie Ross and Barbara Kolk at the AKC for their help with research; to Barbara Jedda McNab, director of the AKC Museum of the Dog, who shared with us images from this amazing collection; and to Bill Secord of the William Secord Gallery, New York, who was always available to answer questions on dogs in art, and who showed us the special treasures in his gallery.

Thanks go to Nic Fulcher and Nicola Allen of the Dog Collar Museum in England for their help and information. And to Laura Bidwa and Rosemary Thurber for their images of the amazing James Thurber. We also thank The Fort Benton River & Plains Society's Schwinden Library and Archives for preserving the legend of Old Shep.

To Judy Keller, who provided photographs of Denis Springer's wonderful bronzes, and to Alison Desmaris of Mirasol Glass Works for sharing her colorful stained glass window of her beloved Yogi. To Stephen Huneck for giving us all a reason to go to the mountain. To Sam Rubin and Geoff Zonder of Yale University for their photos of Handsome Dan. And to Brock Fitzgerald and Purina Farms for sharing their show site.

Thanks to Bowman Hastie and Tillamook Cheddar for their contribution to abstract expressionism. And to Lara Jo Regan and the very special Mr. Winkle for their wonderful, warm, whimsical photographs! The world of art is richer because of you.

A sparkling, diamond-studded thank you to Kris Moyer of The Gilded Paw for providing us with wonderful photos of dogs at their pampered best. Her support of our project and unbridled enthusiasm came at just the right moment! And to Kevin at Happytails for all his help. An extra big biscuit goes to the Three Dog Bakery for making the dog world a more delicious place, and to Barbara's Canine Café for their tasty treats! And thanks to Susan Dinion and Ken Vona for taking dog houses to another level with their Doghouse Lighthouse Birdhouse. And to Linda Sunshine, Willard Carroll, and Toto, too, for their invaluable help.

Special thanks to Dr. Tim Tully for honoring the dogs of Pavlov. They are published here for the first time.

The Collie people turned out to be a truly special group. Thanks go to Marilyn Horowitz of the Terhune Sunnybank Memorial, who provided us with the definitive photographs of Terhune and his dogs, and to Judy Leathers, the national chair of the Sunnybank Memorial. Thanks to Carl Meier, a sensitive and selfless man doing a ton of good work for people in need along with his Collie, Rusty. And thanks to Sue Akin and Donald Fowler for their incredible portraits.

Thanks go to Bill Wynne, Andy Tabar, and Smoky, the Yorkie Doodle Dandy; to Sharon Robinson and the absolutely amazing Chanda-Leah; to Cameron Woo of The Bark magazine; and to Miss Daphne Hereford, who continues the bloodline and protects the heritage of our American hero, Rin Tin Tin. And the world of dogs wouldn't be complete without Barbara and David Hays' staggering collection at Antiquibles!

Thanks to the Golden Retriever Club of America for their information and photo of Guisachan. And to Sue Lavoie and the Ramapo Search and Rescue Dogs for answering hundreds of our questions about their deployments. To Dave and Mary Ray, my good friends in England, who help define the love of dogs with artistry and grace. To John and Tina Spivey of J.T. Pawprints for outstanding agility and flyball photos. They are always in the right place at the right time!

And to all who shared images of their best friends: Robin Siegel, Katherine Ippoliti, George and Libby Peper, Dave Green and Mary Mathwick, Diana Catherines, Milbry, Bill, and Elisabeth Polk, Susan Gerharz, Marian Cannon, Marilyn Degregorio, Gage and Carol Davis, Jana Kolpen, Melinda Barber and Tom Ritchie, Jolene Jackson, Polly and Steve Stetler, Ed Dziuk, Pam and Ken Koehler, Rich Heimbuch, Ahleyah and Reinhart Aberer, John Hughes, Tracie Martyn and Marius Moriau, Cameron Irish, and Barbara Peragine.

To our husbands, Tony Acosta and Hubert Pedroli, who had the patience and humor to see us through one more time. And to our wonderful dogs who make life fun.

319